American Unionism
An Historical and Analytical Survey

D0645996

George H. Hildebrand
Cornell University

/-3341

▲
ADDISON-WESLEY PUBLISHING COMPANY

Reading, Massachusetts ● Menlo Park, California
London ● Amsterdam ● Don Mills, Ontario ● Sydney

PERSPECTIVES ON ECONOMICS SERIES

Michael L. Wachter & Susan M. Wachter, Editors

PUBLISHED

**Development, The International Economic Order
and Commodity Agreements,** *Jere R. Behrman*
**American Unionism: An Historical and Analytical
Survey,** *George H. Hildebrand*
**The Economics of Medical Care:
A Policy Perspective,** *Joseph P. Newhouse*
Money and the Economy: A Monetarist View, *William Poole*
Antitrust Policies and Issues, *Roger Sherman*
Income Distribution and Redistribution, *Paul J. Taubman*

FORTHCOMING

International Trade, *Stephen P. Magee*
Regulation, *Roger G. Noll*
Population, *T. Paul Schultz*
Urban Economics, *Susan M. Wachter*

ISBN 0-201-08368-X
ABCDEFGHIJK-AL-79

Foreword

The PERSPECTIVES ON ECONOMICS series has been developed to present economics students with up-to-date policy-oriented books written by leading scholars in this field. Many professors and students have stressed the need for flexible, contemporary materials that provide an understanding of current policy issues.

In general, beginning students in economics are not exposed to the controversial material and development of current issues that are the basis of research in economics. Because of their length and breadth of coverage, textbooks tend to lack current economic thinking on policy questions; in attempting to provide a balanced viewpoint, they often do not give the reader a feel for the lively controversy in each field. With this series, we have attempted to fill this void.

The books in this series are designed to complement standard textbooks. Each volume reflects the research interests and views of the authors. Thus these books can also serve as basic reading material in the specific topic courses covered by each. The stress throughout is on the careful development of institutional factors and policy in the context of economic theory. Yet the exposition is designed to be accessible to undergraduate students and interested laypersons with an elementary background in economics.

Michael L. Wachter
Susan M. Wachter

Preface

Unions and unionism are not simple or easily comprehended institutions. Yet they play a role of enormous importance in all of the democratic industrial societies—a role that differs from country to country.

Those who would seek to understand American society and its economy of today will find it imperative to have a working knowledge of American unionism. And because American unionism is unique in so many ways, it is essential to know something about its beginnings and its subsequent development if one is to acquire the necessary perspective for understanding it today. Accordingly, the first three chapters of this book are concerned with a brief history of American unionism; the impacts, stemming from the New Deal, of ever-increasing government involvement in union activities; and the important problems and accomplishments of organized labor during the years after World War II. Then, in Chapter 4, the organizational structure of the present American labor movement is set forth.

Proceeding from this background, the book next takes up some major issues of policy posed by unionism and collective bargaining today. One set of questions is concerned with whether particular unions can raise money and real wages; whether some unions are stronger than others, and if so, what are the sources of their exceptional strength?

To enable the reader to deal with these questions, the section sets out with an exposition of some elementary theoretical analysis of the principles of wages and employment at the microeconomic level.

A second set of economic issues—the macroeconomics of unionism, wages, and employment—then follows. Here again some key issues of the day are considered. Do the unions cause inflation, and if so, how? What are their main impacts upon the whole economy? And, now that voluntary wage and price stabilization has just been introduced (in November, 1978) to cope with accelerating inflation, there follows a particularly timely discussion of the problems of stabilization policy.

The third group of issues includes some other topics of basic contemporary importance: unionism and collective bargaining in the government sector, some peculiarities of that sector, the problem of strikes against the government, the impacts of Title VII of the Civil Rights Act of 1964 for unionized labor markets, and the very sensitive question of affirmative action policy and programs.

The book then closes with an analysis of the growth of unionism—the major factors now at work, the areas of strength and weakness, and finally, the prospects that the American labor movement will abandon its traditional approach in favor of policies more typical of Western Europe.

Susan and Michael Wachter have been of much help to me in the preparation of this volume. I am also much indebted to Sara Gamm and George W. Brooks for stimulating discussions and criticism and to Verma McClary for her usual fine job of typing.

February 1979   G. H. H.

Contents

American Unionism, 1
from the 1790s
to the End
of the 1920s

Of the many types of worker organizations to be found among the numerous labor movements around the world, this book will deal with only one: unionism as it has developed in the United States since the 1790s, when it first came into being. Obviously the U.S. movement is among the world's oldest. Also, it has no real counterpart elsewhere.

Unions as they exist in the United States can be described most easily and conveniently as organizations of employees formed to promote certain purposes common to the whole group in their joint status as workers under the direction of those in management. Over the ensuing 175 years since the emergence of the first American unions, their objectives have greatly increased in scope and complexity, while the unions themselves have grown enormously in size and diversity. But in one basic respect they have never changed: they were and they remain employee organizations devoted to the promotion of employee interests. In this endeavor, they have always placed themselves in what for the most part is an adversary relationship to employers. But because this relationship has always rested upon the presupposition of the permanent existence of both sides, typically the opposition between the two has not led to a Marxian type of class struggle for total victory, but rather to a continuing effort of both sides to find a mutually acceptable way to share power in the formulation and administration of the rules of the workplace. This, of course, is but another way of saying that American unionism both accepts and even depends upon the permanence of the system of private enterprise. Its strategy is compromise, not conquest.

UNIONISM IN ITS NONAGE

The earliest American unions were organizations exclusively of craftsmen such as carpenters, printers, and shoemakers—all of trades in which skill and apprenticeship were characteristic from the start. In fact, craft unionism continued to dominate the American labor movement until the historical split of 1935, out of which emerged the CIO as a rival federation of the AFL.

In the beginning, each craft union, or "body" as it was commonly called, was a purely local affair, identified with a particular city or town. Moreover, As Neil Chamberlain has pointed out, these early organizations engaged in no bargaining with their employers (then known as "master workmen"). Yet they were unions. They pursued their interests through the device of unilaterally formulating the terms on which the membership would consent to continue to work. Central to these terms was the list of prices per unit for various product items, such as boots, workshoes, and women's shoes. These prices were the equivalent of the wage-yield expected from the use of standardized tools, techniques, and materials by the journeymen members of the body. To the employing master workman, it was a case of "take it or leave it"; that is, accept the list as formulated or go without the services of the organized journeymen.

This, of course, was not collective bargaining, because it involved no negotiations between buyer and seller. But nonetheless, use of the list was inspired by what were to become the traditional goals of unionism—employee control over wages, hours, and working conditions—backed up by the strike to enforce the terms of the list to be imposed. In modern parlance, this early system readily displays the basic technique permanently employed by American unions from the start: organization of a group of workers having interests in common to act together as a joint group of sellers, to fix wages and other terms of employment such as hours and working conditions, to serve as the exclusive providers of the work to be done, and to regulate the conditions under which newcomers could enter the trade.

Underlying these early ideas of joint action was the principle that a single employee acting alone (journeyman in those days), lacked any effective power to bargain with his employer because he could easily be replaced.

The early craft union members understood full well the principle of acting together, even to the extent of refusing to work alongside of journeymen who had refused to join the body. But in following the principle of joint action, they soon ran afoul of the common-law doctrine of criminal conspiracy—in essence, that an act performed by an individual may be legal, yet become illegal when undertaken in concert by a group of persons. Thus in the landmark Philadelphia shoemakers' case in 1806, a joint action by local shoemakers to impose their list on a "take it or leave it" basis brought about their conviction on a charge of criminal conspiracy [*Commonwealth* v. *Pullis* (1806) in 4, pp. 22, 595]. As the judge then reasoned, the defendants were engaging in "artificial regulation" to replace free competition.

"A combination of workmen to raise their wages," he said, "may be considered in a two-fold point of view: one is to benefit themselves . . . the other is to injure those who do not join their society. The rule of law condemns both . . ." [4, p. 24].

With the passage of time, the conspiracy doctrine was applied to strikes, to refusals to work with nonmembers, and to efforts to force the discharge of journeymen who accepted wages below list [*Commonwealth* v. *Carlisle* (1821); *People* v. *Fisher* (1836) in 4, pp. 25-26]. Then, in a Massachusetts case in 1842, in which conspiracy was charged for refusal to work with nonmembers and compelling their discharge in one instance, the judge concluded unexpectedly that it was not unlawful in principle for a body to try to get all those who worked in an occupation to become members so that it could increase its power. The real test of legality involves the purposes for which the power is to be used. But in leaving the content of the lawful purposes vague, the judge left open the possibility that the strike and other standard forms of joint action were legal after all. In this way, the conspiracy doctrine as applied to labor matters lost force in its original form, although it was to reappear half a century later in connection with the concept of restraint of trade [*Commonwelath* v. *Hunt,* 4 Metcalf 111, 45 Mass. 111 (1843) in 4, pp. 27-29].

EXTENDING THE GEOGRAPHIC REACH OF THE ORGANIZATION

As John R. Commons, one of the great pioneers of the study of American unionism, pointed out long ago, the craft unions were forced to extend their organizational base outward from their original local centers as improved methods of transportation—canals, toll roads, and railroads—widened the product market by cheapening the cost of shipments, which in turn increased the number of sellers in a given market [2, pp. 219-266]. Stated in greatly telescoped form, the widening of the market placed the employers in a given trade in ever greater competition with each other. This pressure in turn led employers to attempt to undercut the union lists and to lower their costs and prices in order to improve their sales position. At the same time, these intensifying competitive forces initiated a gradual change in industrial structure in which the custom-order retail shop began to give way to straight retailing, while production and wholesaling were introduced as specialized functions of their own. Eventually these changes were to bring about the emergence of concentrated and increasingly mechanized production in factories, under conditions in which the traditional master-journeyman relationship became completely obliterated, to be replaced ultimately by factory workers directed by capitalistic employers. With this evolution, a new kind of unionism, with different methods, gradually became necessary.

This historical process, essentially involving the transition from commercial to industrial capitalism, required many decades for its consummation: in shoemaking, for example, the span of change took over three-quarters of the nineteenth century. Moreover, the transition itself actually involved a transformation of methods of production and distribution to those of modern type, while the original journeymen-craftsmen were gradually supplanted by factory workers operating machines. Not all of the craft trades experienced this particular pattern, of course, but similar forces were at work throughout the industrial system.

From the standpoint of unionism and labor relations, particular interest attaches to the effects of a widening product market upon the original local union bodies in each of the various trades. Expansion of the product market brought more and more groups of craftsmen into competition with each other through the link from production costs to sales prices. This confronted the early community-based organizations with a very difficult challenge: either join together with other local unions in the same trade so that lists could be standardized and labor costs put on a regional basis—known to union people as "taking wages out of competition," that is, eliminating them as a differentiating factor in unit cost of the product—or accept destruction as the firms with cheaper labor costs took over the whole market.

The price of survival for unionism in each of the lines of production that already had been organized was to expand along with the market itself, first through regionalization and ultimately by the formation of national bodies, known familiarly as national unions. As this process got under way, organizations known as "city centrals" were also established to bring the various craft unions together in local federations for common local purposes.

Many of these new institutions were wiped out by the economic collapse of 1837. Although the concept of craft unionism remained alive in the 1840s, the labor movement of the time entered a period of experimentation with other techniques of action—in particular, cheap money, free land, and producers' cooperatives. By the end of the decade, the failure of these schemes helped to bring about a return to unionism. Starting with the International Typographical Workers, formed in 1852 as the first permanent national union in the United States, a whole series of national crafts came into being over the next two decades in printing, construction, and railroading.

THE INTRODUCTION OF COLLECTIVE BARGAINING AND OF FEDERATIONS OF UNIONS

We have noted already that during the first half-century of American unionism wages and working conditions were unilaterally imposed on the employer through the list, which in essence constituted an all-or-nothing offer. In 1850, however, Horace Greeley, himself a member of the printers' union in New York City, began contending publicly that "the journeymen should [not] dictate a scale, but they should get the employers to agree to some scale. . . . I admit the right of the employers to participate in the adjustment of the scale . . ." [1, pp. 24-25]. In other words, Greeley wanted the unions to negotiate, not to dictate. As editor of the old *New York Tribune,* he began energetically to promote this principle, while continuing to affirm his belief in unionism as well. However, his words wrought no revolution, and it was not until after the Civil War that the principle of collective bargaining began to replace the tradition of the unilaterally imposed list. Even then the principle did not come into general use until after 1890.

Of equal importance in this period was the emergence of a very different kind of unionism, aimed at social reconstruction rather than either wage fixing or its later variant, collective bargaining. The new organization, known by the imposing name of the Noble Order of the Knights of Labor, was formed in 1869 under the leadership of a tailor by the name of Uriah Stephens as a secret body open to all workingmen without distinction as to craft, occupation, or industry. At the outset, its program was rather vague and altruistic, expressing a need for education concerning labor's fair share of the national income and legislative efforts to "harmonize the interests of labor and capital."

About a decade later, Terence V. Powderly succeeded Stephens as Grand Master Workman. Abandoning secrecy, the order began to push a highly interesting version of the "one big union" idea: all productive labor was to be brought together in a group of producers' and consumers' cooperatives, to end their dependence on private employers and the wage system. In this way the Knights committed themselves to a transformation of economic society itself, in place of the limited and short-run programs of the national unions and their locals. At the same time, the order also began to advocate a surprisingly modern program of labor legislation that included health and safety, equal pay for equal work for both sexes, shorter hours, arbitration of industrial disputes, and abolition of mechanics' lien laws.

In structure, the Knights of Labor was composed of a general national assembly, a group of local assemblies, and several national unions that attached themselves although retaining their independence in all other aspects.[1] Because of diversity among its interest groups and their objectives, the order lacked the cohesion required by the one big union principle. Yet, surprisingly enough, it experienced a brief period of very rapid growth in the mid-1880s. Shortly afterward it lost some critical strikes and then entered a period of quick decline from which it never recovered.

---

1   For a brief account, see Selig Perlman [7, pp. 68-72, 113-118].

During the period of its ascendancy after Powderly took over the leadership, the Knights encountered a rival movement that included some of its own trade union affiliates and that stressed a very different principle of organization. In place of a massive general assembly, these organizations emphasized the doctrine of craft unionism, with a single organization for each occupation or trade. And in contrast with the Knights' goal of a world of cooperatives, the craft group took its departure from the idea of improvement of conditions for its members by practical bargaining with employees for short-run objectives such as wages, hours, and working conditions. In this endeavor, each craft was to have exclusive control over its own affairs, although it would act jointly with its fellow organizations to form a federation to serve their common interests.

The first step was taken in 1881 with the formation of a new national body, the Federation of Organized Trades and Labor Unions, which gathered in the unions of the Knights as affiliates along with some independent ones as well. As a result the new federation acquired some remarkable leaders, headed by Samuel Gompers, all of them deeply committed exclusively to the principle of craft unionism as the sole means of betterment for the American worker. Five years later, these same leaders changed the name of the organization to the American Federation of Labor (AFL), while retaining the same basic ideas that had been developed so long before. Soon afterward the leaders of the AFL displaced the Knights as the spokesmen for organized labor in the United States.

SOME PECULIARITIES ABOUT THE EMERGENCE OF UNIONISM IN THE UNITED STATES

With the advent of the AFL in 1886, there began a period of organizational stability that was to last for nearly half a century, even though it was occasionally briefly upset by passing storms such as the Homestead strike of 1892, the Pullman strike of 1894, the formation of the Industrial Workers of the World (IWW) in 1905, and the great steel strike of 1919.

But before we take leave of the formative period itself, it is of interest to note a few of its outstanding peculiarities. First, American unionism got its start from skilled craftsmen not from factory workers or unskilled laborers. Not the poorest and not the least vocationally prepared, but the best-paid and best-situated workers were the source. In other words, we are not dealing here with the Marxian model—an embittered and increasingly class-conscious proletariat united by its common hatred of all employers and led by an elite determined to overthrow the wage and property system, using trade unions as instruments for the preparation of social revolution.

Second, the early unions were not even open to the unskilled factory worker and were not created to enhance the bargaining power of such workers against the rapidly emerging employers associated with the new industrial society. Quite the contrary. The craft unions were not concerned with factory unionism at all. In each case they based their organization on a particular skill shared by the members, and not on some industrial or extractive product—say, steel or coal—turned out by workers either with all kinds of skills or none at all. Thus it was not the familiar forms of discontent associated with factory production—for example, mechanization, elimination of traditional skilled jobs, or low pay, long hours, and frequent unemployment—that underlay the beginnings of American unionism.

Rather, it would be more accurate to say with Commons [2] that the primary force was the increasing need to protect the standard rates of pay and conditions of work of journeymen in a given trade from the pressures of intensifying competition as product markets began to widen with improving transportation. Thus the journeymen who founded American unionism are probably viewed most accurately as akin to independent businessmen who contracted to supply their skilled services to master workmen under uniform competitive conditions, in the same spirit of acquisitiveness and property-mindedness as the master workman and merchants of the time. Thus they organized craft unions whose geographic scope was adequate to enforce common standards of wages so that there would be no "unfair" competition within their market. Then, as the market widened with improved transportation, the craft organizations found it essential to broaden their own scope and ultimately to join the local groups in a particular craft to form a national union for the trade.

Their method worked, although the courts looked askance at it and it often ran afoul of the common law, that is, the unwritten customary law that in this instance included the principle that strikes and refusals to work together with nonmembers were violations of the prohibition against criminal conspiracies; hence those who participated in such activities were subject to fines and imprisonment. However, for various reasons, mostly economic, it proved impossible to establish permanent national unions during the difficult first half of the nineteenth century. In the 1850s, permanent organizations finally began to appear, and for the first time the principle of collective bargaining began to be considered as an alternative to the simpler craft concept.

Still, the most peculiar fact of all about the four decades following the mid-1800s is the continued dominance of the craft or occupational type of national union, on the principle of one for each skilled trade. Such unions have been described as "horizontal" organizations that in each case claimed title to a particular skilled job—say, millwright (carpenters) or pipe fitter (plumbers)—in whatever industry it might be required. This concept, known technically as the principle of exclusive jurisdiction, involved inclusion of incumbents in the trade and exclusion of all others, whether skilled or unskilled. Thus the American unions based themselves upon the notion of property ownership of the job and the skill required for its exercise. In effect, the members "owned" their trade, regulated it, and determined who could engage in it and who could become an apprentice to train for eventual entry into it [8].

A PERIOD OF STABILITY: 1886-1929

Endowed as it was with its peculiar inheritance of craft unionism, the AFL acquired its own inevitable institutional destiny. In the first place, it was composed exclusively of craft unions, each intensely jealous of its jurisdictional "rights," that is to say, that portion of skilled job territory that the organization claimed for its own "job property." This principle of the exclusive juridsdiction of the national union, as Sumner Slichter once called it, had as its logical correlate a second concept, the principle of autonomy, which has at its core the idea "that national unions should be subordinate to no strong and centrally guided agency, but should be left free to manage their own affairs . . ." [9, pp. 8-10]. Taken together, the doctrines of exclusive jurisdiction and of autonomy meant that the new federation would be loosely knit, limited in functions, and quite subservient to the power of its constituent national unions. By analogy, it was a case of the Articles of the Confederation rather than the principle of Federal Union.

By the 1890s the principle of negotiation or of collective bargaining with employers had largely displaced the original unilateral technique of the "list," a fundamental change that Slichter viewed as completing the doctrinal trinity that was to provide conceptual unity to the AFL for some forty years.[2] Also, by the 1890s a few new national unions of a new structural type had started to appear: the Brewery Workers, the United Mine Workers, the Western Federation of Miners, and the old United Garment Workers. In these organizations, jurisdiction was based not upon a particular skill, which was impracticable, but upon the industry itself and potentially all of its employees, whatever their jobs. Put a little differently, the job territory in these organizations was defined by industry and product group, on a vertical basis, while the union itself was open to all wage workers in the industry, regardless of skill. Thus it is correct to say that the principle of industrial unionism was coterminous with the very earliest years of the AFL. But it is equally accurate to assert that industrial unions at the time were few in number and small in relative importance of membership. For these reasons, their influence within the federation was negligible. Craft unionism was clearly the order of the day and was to remain so until the 1930s.

Yet there was a notable exception, for it was in the early 1890s that Eugene V. Debs quit the Switchmen's Union, a railroad craft, in the

---

2   The principle of the "list" is identical in principle to what is termed a "cartel" in theoretical economics. In both instances, an exclusive and excluding organization is required that by itself determines price and other conditions of sale, and enforces these standard terms on all participants.

conviction that evolving American industrialism called for industrial union-ism—for example, one big union instead of the twenty-odd crafts on the roads. This led him to form the American Railway Union (ARU) in a challenge to all of the railroad crafts. However, the ARU was defeated and destroyed in 1894, when it was forced by a 15 percent wage cut to strike against the very powerful Pullman Company. This experience was drastic enough to cause Debs to give up all hope for unionism and collective bargaining in any form and to turn to socialism as the way forward for the American workingman [3]. With Debs out of the picture, it was Gompers and the AFL who were to set the pattern for American unionism for the next 40 years.

As we have seen, this pattern was based upon four fundamental ideas: craft unionism, autonomy for each national body, exclusive jurisdiction for each national body, and collective bargaining as the exclusive method for social and economic change. Thus there was no real room here for a vigorous program of political action on behalf of labor legislation because the AFL was not a united political force. What politics it practiced were essentially negative in thrust. In other words, the basic problem was to keep the government out of the labor market and out of union affairs, not to bring it in. It was for the unions themselves to advance their members' interests, through the method of direct bargaining. Accordingly, the AFL had no interest in socialism or any kind of labor party. On the contrary, it preached the gospel of nonpartisanship.

In addition, the very principle of autonomy required that the real power would lie with the member national unions. Indeed, the AFL itself had been deliberately designed for weakness, created largely as a device to coordinate the nationals for defense against any incursions by the Knights of Labor or successors of similar type such as the IWW. Accordingly, the federation was to do no bargaining and was not to interfere with the internal affairs of its member unions.

Ideas, of course, have their consequences, and the principles that gave conceptual expression to the federation, its policies, and its institutions throughout the long period after 1886 contained a fascinating paradox. On the one side, as Selig Perlman has forcefully argued, this system of ideas enabled the American labor movement to solve what undoubtedly was its most difficult problem, that of staying permanently organized after nearly a century of failure by the AFL's predecessors. In short, the AFL was a pragmatic success. Its methods worked. In the language of Social Darwinism, the federation was a successful adaptation to the difficult American environ-ment. In consequence it could survive.

On the other side, as Norman J. Ware and other critics have noted, one could contend equally easily that the AFL in fact was an historical anachro-nism whose very success demonstrated its organizational failure. From 1880 onward, the growth of the American economy had been centered in mechanized industry and the large-scale corporate enterprise. Mechanization of the factory system tended to wipe out established skills and to concentrate the work force in jobs involving machine feeding and tending; assembling; moving materials, parts, and finished products; and other tasks typically calling for little skill, although some skills, indeed, often in new forms, continued to be required. At the same time, factory production was usually fragmented in departments and characterized by diverse job structures. Viewed as a whole, these work groups were not easily susceptible to organization through stratification according to a particular skill, although this approach was essential if the existing craft unions were to organize the industrial sector in significant degree without altering their established jurisdictions. At the same time, any attempt to split up the plant work force into a series of craft stratifications would have made it that much easier for any corporate employer, operating from interior lines, so to speak, to fight off organizing campaigns by the particular crafts involved, whether they were acting either singly or in alliance. This lesson was forcefully driven home by the collapse of the steel strike in 1919, which had to be conducted by an alliance of craft unions.

Thus the dominance of the AFL by craft unionism *did* make the organization an historical anachronism. It was well equipped to hold its own in those industries in which the traditional skill groups were already strong—such as construction, printing and publishing, the metal trades, and the railroads. In this sense, it was a success. But in the large new industries in which technological change was particularly active—steel, chemicals, utilities, metal fabrication, automobiles, and so on—the craft unions were unprepared ideologically or in structure to design organizing campaigns whose very feasibility would depend upon acceptance of the principles of industrial unionism. Thus, even by 1900, Slichter says, less than one-tenth of the industrial wage workers had been organized [9, p. 5]. According to Millis and Montgomery [6, pp. 66, n.1, and 82, n.2] the books of the Knights of Labor indicated 700,000 members in 1886, to which they add a "possible" 300,000 unionists belonging to the AFL and independent unions. By 1900, total union membership was estimated by Wolman at 868,500, of which 548,321 were attributed to the AFL [6, Table 1, p. 83; data taken from 12, p. 16]. Indeed, if the 700,000 members "on the books" of the Knights in 1886 are taken at face value, then in fact actual total membership declined by some 130,000 during the first 14 years of AFL dominance. In these respects, then, the AFL was an apparent failure.[3]

3   Mention should be made of the challenge posed by the IWW, founded in 1905 as a classwide organization that also advocated industrial unionism for its component groups. Two prominent unions did affiliate with the IWW—the Machinists and the Western Federation of Miners—only to withdraw within a short time, leaving the IWW as a very small organization based on harvest hands, timber workers, sailors, and longshoremen. Although originally organized by socialists, its basic ideas were syndicalist, with some infusion of Marxism as well.

But while craft union principles continued to be a principal obstacle to the introduction of unionism into the emerging new industries associated with the transition from merchant capitalism and petty manufacturing to the age of big industry and financial capitalism, it would be a gross misreading of the evidence to infer that, with its ascendance, the AFL ushered in a period of complete stagnation. Between 1897 and 1914, for example, total union membership actually increased from 447,000 to 2,687,000, or by six-fold, while the membership of the AFL alone soared from 264,000 to 2,020,000, or by almost eight-fold. Moreover, by 1914 the federation could claim over 75 percent of all union members. Nevertheless, even by 1920 only 11.8 percent of the civilian labor force and 18.9 percent of all nonagricultural employees belonged to unions [11]. More important, the growth of membership after 1904, say Millis and Montgomery, is more to be attributed to growth in the size of existing unions than to extension of the principle of unionism into new industrial territory [6, p. 84]. Thus over half the total increase between 1897 and 1914 was concentrated among the coal miners, the railroad workers, and those in the construction trades; except for the miners, "the great mass of semiskilled and unskilled workers remained unorganized" [6, p. 85].

Beyond the limitations imposed by craft unions, growth in membership was impeded seriously by other factors outside of AFL control: the con-tinuing flood of immigrants (initially a very difficult group to organize); the spread of industry southward and westward into regions often beyond the reach of unionism; and the militant and legally unhampered opposition of large employers to any form of union recognition. The centers of growth in the American economy seemed immune to conquest, even if the federation had dared to contemplate so difficult an undertaking.

Yet World War I was by no means a period of stagnation. Mainly using Wolman's data, Millis and Montgomery estimate that between 1914 and 1920, total union membership rose by 2,361,000, almost doubling the 1914 figure. Over the same years, the AFL gained 2,058,000 members, reaching a total membership of slightly more than twice the 1914 base [6, p. 132].

However, this substantial growth also, as in 1897-1914, was not marked by significant encroachment into new job territory, and for the same reason reflected no impressive development of industrial unionism. As of 1910, Wolman estimates that union membership embraced only 5.8 percent of all employees, and 10 percent of all nonagricultural employees. By 1920, as previously noted, these relative shares had jumped to 11.8 and 18.9 percent, respectively [12, p. 116; 6, pp. 132-133]. But at the same time, Wolman finds for 1910 that 75 percent of all union membership was in craft organizations, as against 78 percent in 1920 [12, p. 92; 6, p. 134, n.2]. In short, the wartime growth of membership was intensive, not extensive. It was concentrated mostly in industries that long had been bastions of trade unionism: construc-tion, the metal and machine trades, shipbuilding and transportation.

With the onset of the 1920s, even intensive growth was destined to
cease, although once the sharp depression of 1921-22 was over it was to be
followed by well-sustained prosperity and expansion until the great crash in
October 1929. In 1920, Wolman estimates union membership at 5,048,000,
of which 4,079,000 belonged to AFL unions [12, p. 16; 6, p. 163]. For 1922
the comparative totals are 4,027,000 and 3,196,000. As of 1929, these
respective totals had fallen to 3,443,000 in the aggregate and 2,961,000 for
the AFL alone. Thus the overall total had declined 14.5 percent during the
boom years, while the AFL group had dropped 7.3 percent.[4]

The end of the period of stability came with the end of the decade
itself—with the onset of the Great Depression. Except for the sharp downturn
in the business cycle in 1921, average real wages overall increased during
the 1920s. Paradoxically, this very fact tended to weaken the appeal of
unionism. Moreover, a strong case can be made that the failure of unionism
to grow during these years in considerable part may be attributed to the
craft structure and outlook of the AFL. Indeed, one of the leading students
of the federation, the late Philip Taft, had the following to say:

> In the twenties the labor movement was completely unified. Even the
> dissonant cries of the I.W.W. and Communists barely reached a whisper.
> Yet we find that it is a decade without progress, without a single
> permanent contribution to the cause or organization of labor [10,
> p. 16].

This is a bit too strong. For while the AFL was not equipped by doctrine
to mount a drive for industrial unionism, it must also be borne in mind that
in this period the employers were free under the law to engage in relatively
unrestrained union busting and resistance to organization. Thus from almost
the moment that the war ended, many employers abruptly terminated their
toleration of collective bargaining, going on the offensive with an anti-union
movement known as the "American Plan," whose principal ingredients were
nonrecognition or withdrawal of recognition of unions and discharge of
employees who led or joined them. A more sophisticated version involved
employee representation plans in which the employer himself organized,
supported, and controlled the body, which engaged in no collective bargaining and had no ties to the independent labor movement. At the same
time, this was also the period in which the Scientific Management doctrines
of Frederick W. Taylor came into vogue, through the introduction of time-
and-motion study, piece rates, and job evaluation, all under management
initiative and control.

Finally, to formulate a comprehensive judgment about the impact of
unionism throughout the period, we must also consider the unionized sector

---

4   For 1930 Wolman estimates total membership, excluding Canada, at 3,073,000,
while the Bureau of Labor Statistics puts the figure at 3,401,000.

of the economy as such. Small though it was, it was of clear importance in fields such as construction, printing and publishing, coal mining, and the railroads. In these fields it brought a new form of regulation of the employer and the workplace, and with it certain protections to its members. In this period there is broad agreement among experts that unionism also raised the average wage of all union workers relative to the average for all nonunion workers. H. Gregg Lewis doubts that unionism at the time contributed a wage advantage of more than 25 percent, while the weighted average for other studies suggests about 18 percent [5, p. 464]. Although this wage advantage apparently was not a widening one except in a depressed period such as 1921, it does seem to have been permanent throughout the 1920s.[5]

Thus we cannot count unionsim as a failure in the 1920s. We can say only that it was relatively small in scale, existed in a hostile political environment, and showed no capacity for innovations that might have strengthened its position to some degree.

REFERENCES

1. Chamberlain, Neil W., and James W. Kuhn. *Collective Bargaining.* 2d ed. New York: McGraw-Hill, 1965.

2. Commons, John R. "American Shoemakers, 1684-1895." In *Labor and Administration.* New York: Macmillan, 1913.

3. Ginger, Ray. *The Bending Cross: A Biography of Eugene Victor Debbs.* New Brunswick, NJ: Rutgers University Press, 1949.

4. Gregory, Charles O. *Labor and the Law.* 2d ed. New York: W. W. Norton, 1961.

5. Lewis, H. Gregg. "Unionism and Relative Wages in the United States." In *Readings in Labor Market Analysis,* edited by John F. Burton, Jr., *et al.* New York: Holt, Rinehart and Winston, 1971.

6. Millis, Harry A., and Royal E. Montgomery. *Organized Labor.* New York: McGraw-Hill, 1945.

7. Perlman, Selig. *A History of Trade Unionism in the United States.* New York: Macmillan, 1929.

8. —————. *A Theory of the Labor Movement.* New York: Macmillan, 1928.

9. Slichter, Sumner H. *The Challenge of Industrial Relations: Trade Unions, Management and the Public Interest.* Ithaca, NY: Cornell University Press, 1947.

10. Taft, Philip. "The Problem of Structure in American Labor." *American Economic Review* 27, No. 1 (March 1937):16.

---

5   This does not mean that unionized workers started with a zero advantage in 1920, and gained all of 18 or 25 percent by 1929. To a considerable extent, they already had a wage advantage before 1920.

11. Troy, Leo. *Trade Union Membership, 1897-1962.* Occasional Paper 92. New York: National Bureau of Economic Research, 1965, 2 (Canadian membership is excluded).

12. Wolman, Leo. *Ebb and Flow in Trade Unionism.* New York: National Bureau of Economic Research, 1936.

From the   2
Great Depression
to the End
of the 1930s

THE CONSEQUENCE OF ECONOMIC COLLAPSE, 1929-1933

The first full year of the great downturn, 1930, was in fact a typical repetition of the familiar cyclical decline in production, employment, and income—certainly less severe than that of 1921.

The real difficulties began with 1931 and were associated with one of the greatest forced liquidations in American history. Behind this catastrophe lay a collapse in the international gold standard, coupled with a drastic shrinkage in the domestic money supply. Contraction continued unabated into the spring of 1932, when a temporary check was accomplished by a brief recourse to open-market purchasing by the Federal Reserve. Still further decline soon followed, accompanied by the collapse of many banks. Finally, the bottom was reached with the forced closure of all the banks in March 1933.

At the time that the country was entering this dismal period, the leaders of the AFL, of course, were the principal spokesmen for organized labor. Among the best known of them were President William Green, Secretary John P. Frey, and Matthew Woll, president of the Photo Engravers. All of them accepted without question the system of private enterprise. Not for nothing, and not in denigration either, could their outlook be described as "business unionism" or "organizational laissez-faire." It was a unionism oriented to the control of the labor market through the collective agreement. It had no political program beyond keeping the government out of the affairs of organized labor.

Today such ideas seem naive and simple. Yet it must be remembered that they had served the federation well for nearly half a century. More than this, the critic should bear in mind that the AFL lacked both the stature and the political influence to divert itself to a different kind of policy. About the

15

most it could do was to resist stubbornly the growing pressure for wage cuts as the depression grew worse. Indeed, under its long-established principle of autonomy for the national union the real power in the American labor movement lay with these organizations, while the federation served mainly as a spokesman on the few general matters of common interest to the nationals.

Taken as a whole, organized labor accounted only for 11.6 percent of all nonagricultural employees in 1930, when its total American membership was only 3.4 million in a civilian labor force of 50 million [4]. By 1933 membership had dropped to only 2,689,000, a decline of nearly 21 percent from 1930. Then, at the very nadir of modern union history, two events of seismic scale completely altered the entire landscape of American labor: the New Deal and an internal split within the AFL itself.

SOLUTION BY SCHISM: THE STRUCTURAL PROBLEM OF THE AMERICAN LABOR MOVEMENT[1]

The deep depression and the pro-unionism and collective bargaining approach of the new Roosevelt administration undoubtedly awakened a friendly reception among millions of industrial workers who had never been organized—so much so that a rash of strikes broke out in early 1933, followed by the formation of small industrial unions, particularly in the automobile industry, in part by the breakaway of organizations formerly operating under employee representation plans. All of these new organizations were independent of the nationals in the federation.[2]

It can hardly be denied that particularly in this boiling context craft unionism indeed *was* a problem. First, the principle of autonomy denied to the federation itself and to its executive council much freedom of initiative either in chartering unions of the industrial type or in undertaking organizing campaigns in their behalf. Second, the principle of exclusive jurisdiction reserved certain job territory to the existing crafts, even in industries toward which they had never shown a scintilla of interest and in which the craft structure could only have been applied at the cost of completely excluding the unskilled and semiskilled from the benefits of any organization and collective bargaining at all. Yet these paper claims of the crafts were a basic obstacle to industrial unionism because these bodies controlled the executive council and could block any initiatives from within the AFL to issue new union charters. At the same time, with good reason the craft leaders viewed the formation of industrial unions as a threat, because such organizations

---

1   For a thorough account of the AFL-CIO controversy, see Walter Galenson [1].

2   Much of the following discussion relies upon Millis and Montgomery's extensive account of these times, along with Philip Taft's pioneering paper on the structural problem. Cited as [2] *and* [3].

could challenge as well as encroach upon the crafts' jurisdictions, and eventually even might capture majority power within the federation itself.

Third, craft unionism for decades had stood for the principle of voluntarism, a somewhat subtle concept among whose elements were the notions that unions will emerge by themselves, when the workers want them, and that the typical basis for such initiatives is the sharing of a common skill; indeed, that a shared skill is the only basis for an enduring national union—a view that excluded the unskilled and semiskilled workers entirely. In other words, "voluntarism" was but an aspect of the principle of craft unionism itself, while in application it meant that industrial unionism was impractical, that the unskilled could never successfully be organized. On this negative premise, the executive council in 1933 found itself committed to the status quo.[3]

But this commitment did not mean that the AFL would—or could—stand still. Its executive council was being besieged to issue industrial union charters from the start of 1933. With the advent of the National Industrial Recovery Act (NRA) and its promise of collective bargaining in the famous Section 7(a), the pressure increased even further.

The executive council's response was an ingenious one. Addressing itself to the task of organizing the automobile workers, it provided in a directive that "each plant will be organized into a federal labor union under a charter granted by the American Federation of Labor" [3, p. 8]. This declaration was absolutely fatal to industrial unionism for several reasons. The organizations were to be formed on a plant-by-plant basis and thus would be isolated from each other, although they would have to deal with multiplant companies. Still worse, these plant unions in fact would be federal labor locals, chartered by the federation, dependent for leadership, funds, and policymaking upon the craft-dominated executive council. And finally, there was nothing to prevent the applicable crafts from exercising their jurisdictional rights to pick off members from these helpless locals, leaving a residue of unskilled or semiskilled workers bereft of any national industrial union to protect and promote their interests.

This approach posed the basic issue in the whole controversy: Were the mass-production industries to be organized by national industrial unions chartered and supported by the AFL, or were these workers either to be passed over or to be picked over by the crafts after having been confined to isolated plant locals?

---

3   As Taft points out, the AFL leaders from the 1880s were aware that the craft principle would be a problem because it led to jurisdictional inflexibility, unresponsiveness to technological change, and inherent hostility to all industrial unionism. Various efforts to resolve the question thus became a necessity through the years: widening the jurisdictional base, merger of crafts, and the formation of special departments to bring related crafts together to deal with joint interests and problems [3, pp. 4-6].

The issue was joined in the AFL convention in San Francisco in October 1934. At this point an effort was made to reach a compromise: craft rights were to be fully protected; the executive council was to issue industrial union charters for the automobile, aluminum, and cement industries; the federation was to launch an organizing campaign in steel; and the new organizations would be under federation control. This measure was adopted probably because its very ambiguities supplied a measure of comfort to both sides.

Unfortunately, the AFL leadership soon lost even this much zeal. Months went by without any significant official action. By the time of the next convention, in Atlantic City in the fall of 1935, the industrial unionists were ready with a vigorous minority report on behalf of their cause: the present craft unions would be left untouched and where this mode of organization was even "potentially" workable, it would be respected. But where industrial unionism was the only solution, leadership and organization would be provided.

The report was rejected. Instead, executive council policy was endorsed: present industrial unions were to be left undisturbed, but the jurisdictional interests of the crafts were to be fully protected.

The schism was now out in the open. Conferences began immediately among the industrial unionists, and on November 10, 1935, the Committee for Industrial Organization (CIO) was formed[4] under the leadership of John L. Lewis, president of the United Mine Workers.[5] The declared purpose of the CIO was to encourage and promote the organization of mass-production workers "upon an industrial basis," but without "injury" to existing national unions, although the new body was also "to modernize the organization policies" of the AFL [2, p. 211].

The response of AFL President William Green was a series of indignant and yet restrained attacks on the CIO; by July 1936, Secretary John P. Frey was charging it with "dualism, rebellion, fomenting insurrection." A private trial was scheduled, but the defense failed to show up. It was busily engaged in setting up organizing committees in the basic industries. Suspension of the existing CIO nationals followed, although this was tempered by an AFL

---

4   A somewhat less idealistic motive for Lewis has been suggested: that he needed an industrial union in steel to bring that industry's captive coal mines into collective bargaining so that the Mine Workers would have less low-cost competition to confront where a common product was involved.

5   The original CIO had the following participating organizations: the United Mine Workers, the Amalgamated Clothing Workers, the International Ladies Garment Workers, the United Textile Workers, the Oil Field, Gas Well, and Refinery Workers, and the International Union of Mine, Mill, and Smelter Workers. In addition, the CIO had the Cap and Millinery Department of the United Hatters; while Charles P. Howard, president of the International Typographical Workers, joined personally, without his organization.

effort at settlement. This attempt failed. Early in 1937 the CIO unions were expelled from the AFL.

Then, in October 1937, the CIO proposed a conference with the AFL. The offer was accepted, and at a meeting on October 25 an oral compromise apparently was reached in response to separate proposals from each side. Under the formula, which came from the AFL group, (1) the old national unions that had affiliated with the CIO, now numbering 12, would not rejoin the federation until all issues involving the 20 additional new CIO organizations had been resolved, including jurisdictional questions; (2) at this point all 32 CIO unions would return to the AFL; (3) a special convention would then be held, at which a list of industries appropriate for industrial unionism would be developed; and (4) no charter would be revoked except in convention. Taken as a whole, the AFL solution seemed moderate and workable, particularly since the CIO delegation initially accepted it. Nonetheless, the CIO group repudiated the understanding the very next day, presumably under pressure from Lewis, on the justification that the AFL representatives had refused to agree to prepare the industry list then and there, a step they were not authorized to take. Behind these labyrinthine maneuvers lay the central fact that because the CIO now enjoyed the momentum of rapidly spreading success, its leaders were reluctant to abandon a winning strategy; yet at the same time, they found it inexpedient to adopt a public position in opposition to all efforts at reconciliation.

By January 1938 the federation began revoking the charters of the original "rebel" unions. However, both the International Typographical Workers and the United Hatters were exempted. Also, the International Ladies Garment Workers Union subsequently left the CIO and made its return. By fall 1938 the committee had converted itself to a federation under the title Congress of Industrial Organizations. The schism was now complete; the nation now had two rival federations, each now vigorously engaged in organizing campaigns.

In 1939 another attempt at reconciliation was made at the intercession of President Roosevelt. At this conference, Lewis proposed the formation of a new federation, with equal representation for both sides on the executive council; he and Green were to withdraw as possible candidates for president. The AFL responded by reiteration of its 1937 proposal of settlement. Nothing was resolved. In fact, 16 years would pass before the two bodies could achieve merger.

So far, our account of these events has pointed to factors such as the conflict between the craft and the industrial union principles and between the leaders of the two factions. And, indeed, both factors were powerful influences throughout the critical early years of the split. But there were other less obvious but equally powerful forces also at work.

One was the Great Depression, which did so much to destroy faith in the existing economic system, and which thereby lent great strength to

Roosevelt's program of intervention and regulation, in particular his support for expansion of unionism and collective bargaining. Soon this support was to turn into statutory form, with the Wagner Act of 1935.

Beyond these political factors, the depression laid bare the inadequacy of the craft principle of union organization. Ever since the end of the Civil War, the American economy had been undergoing a major transformation from small commercial enterprises and craft trades to mechanized factory production largely managed by corporations, large and small. The evolution of this new system brought about a factory form of labor force, a great diversity in occupations and in types and degrees of skills. In many industries, it also gave rise to the multiplant employer.

Economic and technological change simply made craft unionism increasingly obsolete as time went on. If organized labor was to grow with the country, it simply had to reconstruct its own organizational doctrine to incorporate the principles of industrial unionism. This was a concession that the national crafts were unwilling to make. For the same reason, the leaders of the AFL lacked both the authority and the initiative to make it themselves. Accordingly, when the New Deal gave the big push to unionization, the AFL and its affiliates were neither prepared nor willing to seize the opportunity. Both the schism and the CIO were the result.

THE NEW DEAL AND THE UNIONS

Just as the close of the Hoover administration turned out to be the end of the long period of limited central government in the United States, it also marked the end of the period of "do-it-yourself" nonpartisan unionism. Put differently, the new Roosevelt administration was strongly interventionist from the start, while the labor market and labor-management relations were very much a part of that intervention.

There were precedents, of course. The railroad industry had always been treated as a special case, starting with the Erdman Act of 1898. In 1931 Congress passed the Davis-Bacon Act to regulate construction wages on projects involving federal funds. And in 1932 the Norris-LaGuardia Act was adopted to limit the use of federal injunctions in labor disputes. More precisely, the object of Norris-LaGuardia was statutory intervention to get the federal courts out of ordinary labor disputes. In this sense its aim was to reduce intervention by the federal judiciary, in keeping with the classical AFL philosophy.

Of all the New Deal legislation, the measure of greatest importance to organized labor was the National Labor Relations (Wagner) Act of 1935. The act made it illegal for employers to oppose unionism or to interfere with unions already established, and it required employers to recognize and to bargain collectively with unions chosen by majority vote to represent the employees involved.

The law takes as its point of departure the principle that the employers who deny their employees the right to bargain collectively thereby promote strikes and labor unrest and in this way impose a burden upon the free flow of interstate commerce. It also proclaims that the inequality of bargaining power between the employer and the single employee depresses wages and purchasing power, and through both brings about depressions.

Thus in Section 7 the law asserts the principle of full freedom of association among workers by assuring them the right to form, join, and organize unions without interference. To effectuate this right, the act sets forth in Section 8 five types of unfair labor practices that are proscribed for employers:

1. Interference with the rights affirmed in Section 7.
2. Domination or interference with the formation or administration of unions.
3. Discrimination against members of unions either in hiring or tenure of employment.
4. Discharge or discrimination against an employee for filing charges under the act.
5. Refusal to bargain collectively with a union certified to represent a majority of the employees in a bargaining unit.

On the administrative side, the National Labor Relations Board (NLRB) was set up, consisting of three members and an apparatus of field examiners, lawyers, and trial examiners organized in a system of regional offices.

The law assigned to the board two main functions: those involving complaints alleging unfair labor practices and those concerned with "certification" of unions to represent employees in collective bargaining. Complaint cases at that time in the history of the act originated, of course, from charges against employers alleging violation of one or more of the unfair labor practices cited above. In essence, the procedure in complaint cases was to conduct a hearing to determine whether the evidence sustained the charge, and if it did in the judgment of the board, then to devise an appropriate remedy imposed by order. Typically the remedy might involve reinstatement of discharged employees with back pay or a directive to an employer to meet with a union and engage in good-faith bargaining looking toward an ultimate agreement. And although the test of "good faith" is not always an easy one, the board from the start has never taken the position that the employer *must* make a contract to be in good faith. The reason is obvious: free collective bargaining must allow for the possibility of *impasse,* for an ultimate disagreement followed by a strike or lockout. Parties can not be compelled to make a contract; they can only be required to try to do so.

As for the representation function of the board, it is the means by which the NLRB determines whether a group of employees wish to be represented by some particular union for collective bargaining. The process starts with a petition by a group of employees—now 30 percent—asking for a representation election.[6] The next step is for the board to determine the boundaries of the job territory that is to compose the voting district for the representation election. This is usually termed the designation of a unit appropriate for purposes of collective bargaining. These voting units may be based on a particular craft, or they may be comprised of both craft and production workers in what is often called a "production and maintenance" (p. and m.) unit. Moreover, the unit may consist of only part of a plant, an entire plant, or even a group of plants, according to the particular case.

Once the voting district is designated, the next step is the election itself. Here the general rule is that the voters must have "no union" as one of the choices before them. Then the majority preference among those voting decides the outcome. If there is no such preference, a runoff is held for the two highest options. In the upshot, if a contending union is the majority choice, then the board "certifies" the organization as the collective bargaining representative for all employees in the original voting district, which now becomes the "bargaining unit." Obviously the representation procedure made organizational strikes unnecessary and at the same time effectuated the employees' fundamental right under the act to decide by majority vote which union, if any, they wished to have negotiate labor agreements for them.

More by coincidence than intent, the Wagner Act became law just before the CIO came into being. By mid-1936, Lewis was ready to open the drive to organize basic steel. The next two and a half years witnessed the most rapid growth of union membership in American labor history up to that time.

The CIO factor is important because the bitterness on both sides of the split between the CIO and the AFL embroiled the new NLRB in controversy almost from the start, particularly for its design of bargaining units, which the AFL charged with growing insistence reflected a pro-CIO policy. By 1940 the AFL was urging that the Wagner Act itself be repealed mainly for this reason, and the Roosevelt administration found it expedient to reconstitute the board and its membership to placate the AFL critics as well as those from business who viewed the NLRB as systematically biased against them in all of its activities.

The real significance of the Wagner Act for American unionism can hardly be overemphasized. It threw the whole power of the federal government behind the worker's right to organize and to have collective bargaining. This was accomplished in two ways. First, the right of full freedom of association was backed up by a representation procedure based upon majority vote. Second, employers now had the duty to bargain collectively

---

6   By the same means, a group can petition for an election looking toward the termination of representation by a union.

when the majority preference was in support of a particular union. More than this, employers also were enjoined by law, in the unfair labor practices clause, from all actions intended to frustrate or deny the right of freedom of association created by the new statute. Thus in one giant step the federal government moved from nonintervention to detailed intervention into labor relations policy, on behalf of employees and collective bargaining.

It should also be noted that through the election and certification procedure the act also gave legal sanction to the traditional AFL doctrine of exclusive representation—in essence, only one union could bargain for a given work group, a provision that reduced raiding and organizational disruptions.

Because the Wagner Act preceded the CIO organizational drive by hardly more than a year, it is impossible to assess with precision their relative importance in adding new union members. Table 2.1 indicates their combined influence.

Table 2.1   Union membership, 1936-44 (in thousands).

Year	AFL	CIO	Total[a]	Change in Total
1936	3,516.4		4,107.1	
1937	3,179.7	1,991.2	5,780.1	1,673.0
1938	3,547.4	1,957.7	6,080.5	300.4
1939	3,878.0	1,837.7	6,555.5	475.0
1940	4,343.2	2,154.1	7,282.0	726.5
1941	5,178.8	2,653.9	8,698.0	1,416.0
1942	6,075.7	2,492.7	10,199.7	1,501.7
1943	6,779.2	3,303.4	11,811.7	1,612.0
1944	6,876.5	3,037.1	12,628.0	816.3

a.   Includes membership in unaffiliated unions.

Source: Leo Troy, *Trade Union Membership, 1897-1962.* Occasional Paper 92 (New York: National Bureau of Economic Research, 1965), p. 8.

Table 2.1 shows, first, that 1937 was the peak year of the CIO's initial organizing drive, which occurred in peacetime. Second, the table indicates that the AFL quickly began a recovery from its initial loss of members, which was caused mainly by explusions and withdrawals of affiliated organizations. Indeed, between 1938 and 1944, the AFL easily outstripped its rival in growth. Accordingly, one is tempted to conclude that despite its many complaints against the NLRB, the competition supplied by the CIO invoked a prompt and aggressive organizing reaction from the AFL, in which ancient craft doctrines were quickly thrown overboard in the interests of survival.

And finally, apart from the single year of 1937, the big gains were registered during 1941-44, as employment surged under the influence of war and war preparations. Thus it could be inferred that the gains of the late 1930s reflected organizing by breakthroughs into new industrial territory, helped by the Wagner Act. By 1941 and after, internal growth through already established bargaining units had become a major factor, although breakthroughs continued to be prominent, helped by both the NLRB and the War Labor Board.

It would be a mistake to think that the Wagner Act was the sole great political factor affecting organized labor in New Deal times. That it easily headed the list goes without saying. But this was also the period of the Social Security Act, the Unemployment Compensation law, and the Fair Labor Standards Act. Unfortunately, space is lacking to describe those measures here.

REFERENCES

1. Galenson, Walter. *The CIO Challenge to the AFL: A History of the American Labor Movement 1935-1941.* Cambridge, MA: Harvard University Press, 1960.

2. Millis, Harry A., and Royal E. Montgomery. *Organized Labor.* New York: McGraw-Hill, 1945.

3. Taft, Philip. "The Problem of Structure in American Labor." *American Economic Review* 27, No. 1 (March 1937):16.

4. U.S. Department of Labor, Bureau of Labor Statistics. *Directory of National Unions and Employee Associations, 1975.* Bulletin 1937. Washington, D.C.: Government Printing Office, 1977.

From 3
World War II
to the
Present Day

THE IMPACTS OF WORLD WAR II

After the attack on Pearl Harbor brought the United States into the war at the close of 1941, private interests were quickly displaced by the national imperative of winning the conflict by building up the armed forces and along with this the production of armament and war supplies. Starting with these objectives, the Roosevelt administration quickly began to assemble a whole system of direct controls to deal with labor disputes, manpower allocation, rationing of production materials and consumers' goods, and ceilings over prices and wages.

In the area of labor relations, President Roosevelt first brought together the leaders of business and organized labor in a conference at which the famous No Strike—No Lockout pledge was affirmed by both sides and a special system of resolving disputes and controlling wages was endorsed.

The outcome was the formation of the National War Labor Board, (WLB), which acquired the double duty of providing and enforcing dispute settlements without stoppages, and of controlling wages as well. Wage control in its first form involved the "Little Steel" formula (May 1942), which put a "cap" on cost-of-living increases at 15 percent above the level prevailing in January 1941. By 1943 the WLB had also introduced a complex system of wage "brackets" that typically involved prevailing statistical limits above which area job rates in given industries could not be increased. For approximately three years to come, wages were under detailed administrative control by the board. Meanwhile, this agency itself soon became supplemented by twelve regional War Labor Boards, plus some special "commissions" for industries such as construction, motor freight, and newspapers.[1]

---

1 Some flexibility was provided for wage control by allowance of certain increases as exceptions to the brackets—for very low wages, for "gross inequities," and to "aid in the effective prosecution of the war."

The WLB system was administered by tripartite boards involving equal representation for the public, industry, and organized labor.

To carry out its double function of settling disputes and regulating wages, the WLB soon found itself saddled with the task of developing standards for dealing with a great range of issues embracing all major aspects of industrial relations, from wages and fringe benefits to union security. By a combination of patience and ingenuity, backed up by a spirit of national unity invoked by the war, the board accomplished an astonishing success in preventing strikes and lockouts and in holding wage rates within designated guidelines. In part, this achievement rested upon its tripartite structure. In its four-year lifetime, the WLB made some valuable contributions to collective bargaining. Among these were the widespread extension of voluntary arbitration of grievances as a permanent provision in labor-management agreements and the development of the "maintenance-of-membership" device as a resolution of the issue of union security. This issue requires a word of explanation.

Union security concerns the desire of unions to be protected from "dilution" of membership occurring when, with the national turnover of any work force, an employer's hiring policy is to add anti-union employees as much as possible. This problem is particularly acute in casual trades such as construction, where turnover is great. The traditional union solutions to the security problem have been the closed and the union shop. Under a closed-shop clause, the employer must hire only union employees. With a union shop, the employer may hire whomever he or she chooses, but after new employees pass the probationary period (usually 30 days), they must join the union if they are to keep their jobs. Factory unionism normally relies on the union shop.

Most American employers have resisted both systems very strongly. Thus when demands for union security became issues in wartime disputes, the WLB had to resolve the issue in a way that could be acceptable to both its labor and management members. The solution was the "maintenance-of-membership" clause, which provided that (1) each employee in the bargaining unit could vote at the start of a new agreement whether he or she wished to belong to the union and (2) if the decision were affirmative, then the employee had to remain a member in good standing for the life of the agreement.

THE TAFT-HARTLEY ACT

With the end of World War II, wage controls were withdrawn almost immediately. For nearly two years thereafter, the country experienced a flood of strikes, some of which were a very serious threat to production in essential industries.

This strike wave occurred against a background of long-standing complaints against the Wagner Act, mostly emerging from employers. In brief, it was claimed that the act was biased against employers, that it left the unions free of any duty to bargain in good faith, and that the NLRB had been functioning as judge, jury, and prosecutor all in one.[2] Thus the time was ripe for more federal labor legislation.

The Taft-Hartley Act is an omnibus measure of extreme complexity. Accordingly, we can consider only its main elements here. To begin, one of its most important characteristics is that it perpetuates the central concept of the Wagner Act; namely, that it is the task of the federal government *to protect* the right of the worker to join or help form a union, indeed *to encourage* him or her to do so. In the Wagner Act, it was considered essential as well as sufficient to this purpose to introduce a series of restraints and duties to be imposed upon employers alone, mostly by means of a list of "unfair labor practices." In this way workers could have "unions of their own choosing" that, once certified by the NLRB, acquired the right of exclusive representation[3] for collective bargaining, while the employers now had the duty to bargain with these unions in good faith.

In this case, what the Taft-Hartley Act did was to impose a collateral duty on the union also to bargain in good faith; indeed, a union's failure to do so—for example, by refusing to discuss an employer's demand or to deviate in any way from its own initial list of demands—now became an unfair labor practice. But this was only one of many union practices that now became proscribed. All of them may be grouped as follows:[4]

1. Union unfair labor practices involving other unions:[5]
   a) To compel an employer to assign particular work to a given union that has not been certified to represent the employees in the bargaining unit in which the work was involved.
   b) To compel an employer to bargain with some given union when another union has already been certified to represent the bargaining unit involved.
2. Union unfair labor practices involving employers:
   a) To refuse to bargain in good faith (noted above).
   b) To compel or attempt to compel an employer to pay for work not performed or not to be performed.[6]

---

2   In part these and other complaints had been quietly rectified already after 1940 by the board itself, which was now headed by Professor Harry A. Millis of Chicago and two other new members.

3   "Exclusive" until successfully challenged either by another union or through a petition for a "decertification" election.

4   Based upon Sumner H. Slichter [6, pp. 1-31].

5   Both of these practices involve interference with the rights of employees in the bargaining unit.

6   This provision is known as the "anti-featherbedding clause."

    c) To compel an employer to cease handling the products of another employer, or to cease doing business with any person.[7]

    d) To force an employer or independent businessman to join a union.

3. Union unfair labor practices involving employees:

    a) Coercion of employees into joining a union unless it has a union-shop clause or into joining a strike when they wish to continue to work.

    b) Coercion of employees or prospective employees by attempting to induce the employer to discriminate against them for nonmembership in the union unless there is a legal union-shop clause in the agreement.

    c) Coercion of employees by attempting to force the employer to discharge or discriminate against them for reasons other than their failure to pay regular fees and dues under a legal union-shop clause.

    d) Coercion of prospective or actual employees by imposing a closed-shop form of union security, or a union-shop clause not accepted by majority vote of the employees in the unit.[8]

    e) Exaction of "excessive" initiation fees under an agreement containing a union-shop clause.

The Taft-Hartley Act also introduced the concept of strikes and lockouts that are a threat to the health and safety of the public. Under this provision, the President determines whether the threatened stoppage constitutes a national emergency. If he so finds, he may appoint a board of inquiry to investigate and to report without recommendations on the issue, whereupon the President may seek an injunction in federal district court to prevent or to terminate the stoppage. If the court issues the order, the board has 60 days to prepare a full report, after which 15 days remain to take an employee vote, employer by employer, on each employer's last offer of settlement. Within the ensuing five days, the attorney general must request dissolution of the injunction. If the dispute remains unresolved, the President is to submit his report with recommendations to Congress.

Finally, other provisions of the act altered the administrative structure of the NLRB. Its membership was increased from three to five. Its investi-

---

7   This provision is aimed at the "secondary boycott" and "hot cargo clause." The former occurs when employer *B* is struck or picketed to further a dispute not with *B* but with employer *A*. "Hot cargo" involves refusal to transport goods designated by the union to be "hot" (coming from an employer with whom it has a dispute), even though the union had no dispute with the carrier or shipping company handling the goods.

8   The union-shop election provision was abolished by Congress in 1951. Under Section 14(b), the Taft-Hartley Act defers to stricter state laws in matters of union security in which the state statute forbids the union shop, the maintenance-of-membership clause, and/or the "agency shop" (in which a fee may be paid in lieu of dues). These are known as "right-to-work" states.

gative and prosecuting functions were turned over to the general counsel, who was to be appointed by the President and who was to operate the regional offices, while the board confined itself to its judicial function. The general counsel was granted discretion in bringing charges of unfair labor practices, but was required to do so where secondary boycotts were involved.

There remain some other items that can only be noted, although they are essential to round out the discussion. For the first time, employers were allowed to express their views on unions, provided that they made no threats or promises to their employees. Supervisors (foremen) were excluded from the act, while professionals could be included in a bargaining unit only if they consented. Employers were allowed to petition for certification elections and to resort to damage suits where unfair labor practices by unions were involved. Union leaders were required to file non-Communist affidavits, subject to perjury charges; failure to file would deprive their organization of all representation rights under the act. Finally, regulations were introduced covering employer contributions to health and welfare funds, while the checkoff of dues was permitted only by majority vote of the employees. Attempt was also made to regulate union political expenditures.

Taft-Hartley became law in 1947 over President Truman's veto. The act is not beyond adverse criticism in several respects, but this is a topic beyond the scope of this book. In any event, it is clear that the law was the first major step by the federal Congress to bring unions under detailed public regulation, much as it had done with employers in the Wagner Act of 1935. In short, part of the legislative theory of the Taft-Hartley Act was simply that if government was to encourage unionism and collective bargaining, then it also had the duty to make sure that unions acted in the public interest and that the basic rights of employees were protected from interference and coercion by anybody, employers and unions alike.

Put differently, when the federal government began to intervene deeply into labor-management affairs in 1935 for the purpose of encouraging union membership and collective bargaining, it achieved an implicit conversion of unions from private organizations to quasi-public bodies. The principal way in which this was accomplished was through board conferral of certification upon a given union, which involved a significant grant of power to the organization, in particular through the exclusive right to represent the employees in collective bargaining. A dozen years later the Taft-Hartley Act constituted recognition that these grants of power in fact had brought into the open four competing interests or "equities" in industrial life: those of the employees, those of the unions, those of the employers, and those of the public as a whole. This statutory recognition was neither perfect nor was it complete. But it was implicit in the inner logic of the original Wagner Act itself.

A dozen years after the Taft-Hartley Act became law, Congress and the public had been made aware, chiefly through the hearings of the McClellan

Committee in the U.S. Senate, that graft, corruption, racketeering, and dictatorial control were not at all uncommon among unions, at the national, regional, and local levels. These revelations brought out still another major equity: the interests of the members in the conduct of their own unions. To protect these interests more fully, and to correct some of the demonstrated weaknesses of the Taft-Hartley Act, Congress in 1959 passed the Labor Management Reporting and Disclosure Act, commonly known as the Landrum-Griffin law.

THE LANDRUM-GRIFFIN LAW

Title I of the new law assured the members of a union the right to vote by secret ballot in all matters involving dues, fees, and assessments. Each member was also given the right to have a copy of the collective bargaining agreement affecting him or her. Mainly through Title IV, the members became entitled to honest elections: each local was required to hold a secret-ballot election of officers at most every three years, and each national union at most every five years.[9] Through Title II, trusteeships imposed by the nationals upon locals were brought under regulation. Because a trustee-ship involves suspension of control of a local by its local officers, the act sets out the specific purposes for which suspension is legitimate—for example, corruption, dishonesty or racketeering involving local officials. Through this provision, the intent was to eliminate trusteeships whose purpose was to suppress legitimate local opposition to the national leadership. In addition, it was required that the national had to report on trusteeships to the Secretary of Labor, and it was presumed that no trusteeship need last beyond two years to serve any justifiable purpose.

The act also protected the employee's right to be a member of the union on equal terms: a member could not be fined or expelled without a hearing in which he or she had an opportunity to hear and answer the charges against him or her. Every union was required to have a constitution and to file a copy along with financial data with the Secretary of Labor. Employers dealing with unions were required to disclose any loans or other payments to union officers and any payments to labor consultants.[10] In turn, local officers acquired strict fiduciary obligations to their memberships as regards all financial transactions, while members were given the right to sue in court for an accounting as well as restitution of funds upon proof of wrongdoing.

Through Title VII, the new law also incorporated provisions that dealt not with internal union affairs but with various union practices involved in labor disputes. In part these provisions modified earlier ones in the Taft-

---

9   The Department of Labor was given authority to supervise elections and to set them aside where fraud was proved.

10   Certain "consultants" had been revealed to be go-betweens for arranging "sweetheart" deals with crooked union officials. .

Hartley Act. "Hot cargo" clauses were made explicitly illegal except in the construction and apparel industries. Prohibition of secondary boycotts was tightened to eliminate use of direct threats made to an employer by a union official or direct appeals to an individual employee not to handle another producer's products.

Picketing was also brought under added control.[11] Where the purpose is extortion from an employer, it is a federal penal offense. In addition, it was declared to be an unfair labor practice for a union to picket for the purpose of compelling the organization of employees and recognition of a given union at a time when a duly certified union already holds representation rights, or when no associated petition for a representation election has been filed with the NLRB within a period not in excess of 30 days after the picketing has begun. However, the act permitted so-called informational picketing, even where another union has been certified, if the objective is solely to "inform" employees or customers, and not to compel recognition.

To conclude, then, the Landrum-Griffin law opened the way to federal regulation of internal union affairs, most importantly by its bill of rights for members and its fiduciary obligations for officers. Yet it included no protection for blacks and other minorities as regards categorical discrimination against them by unions, or by unions and employers together. This matter had to wait for correction until the Civil Rights Act of 1964.

THE MERGER OF THE AFL AND THE CIO

Undoubtedly, the formation of a new federation, the AFL-CIO, in 1955 was one of the most important events in the history of American labor after World War II. Two developments made the merger possible: the decision in 1949 of the CIO leadership under Philip Murray to put certain unions on "trial" in private proceedings on suspicion of Communist control; and an agreement in 1952 by the leaders of the AFL and CIO not to engage in raiding each other's jurisdictional domains.

As regards the Communist issue, the new CIO policy led to the expulsion of several national unions, among them the International Longshoremen's and Warehousemen's Union on the West Coast and the Mine, Mill and Smelter Workers, as well as some smaller organizations. In addition, the United Electrical, Radio and Machine Workers quit voluntarily. Thus the remaining unions in the CIO were potentially "acceptable" to the more conservative AFL, and were ready for merger when it eventually came.

In November 1952, William Green and Philip Murray died within a few weeks of each other. Meanwhile, John L. Lewis had ceased to be a factor, having taken the Mine Workers on an independent course some time

---

11 "Picketing" involves the tactic of posting a union person or persons near a firm's place of business, usually to discourage its employees from reporting to work or to deter customers from patronizing the establishment.

before. George Meany of the Plumbers, who was secretary-treasurer of the AFL at the time, was chosen to head the senior federation, while Walter Reuther of the Automobile Workers took over as leader of the CIO. The road to merger was now open.

Early in 1953, the two new leaders agreed upon a no-raiding pact. This was an important move, not only for demonstrating mutual good faith and community of interest, but as a practical measure for reducing the jurisdictional rivalries latent in the very existence of the CIO as a competing federation. In this way, the split could be diminished in importance, permitting negotiations to be undertaken.

Then, in February 1955, Meany and Reuther reached agreement in principle upon a merger. Later in that year the two conventions ratified the agreement and merger became a reality.[12] Here is should be noted that a major obstacle was avoided by deliberately putting to one side the even more difficult issue of combining existing rival or overlapping national unions as part of the consolidation of the two federations. Each constituent union, in other words, would be left intact after merger, with freedom thereafter to negotiate or not to negotiate individual mergers with parallel bodies. This took the whole structural issue off the table.

In addition, as we noted earlier in another connection, membership growth had been slowing down following the war, while various organizing drives had failed to win much new ground. In consequence there was growing concern about stagnation among the leaders of the labor movement, and the belief emerged that division had become a weakening agent. Along with this there had developed a parallel conviction that with the Taft-Hartley Act and the various state right-to-work laws, the labor movement badly needed to mobilize and consolidate its forces if it were to move ahead in the unfriendly political atmosphere that it sensed to be forming.

After the new AFL-CIO had come into being, with George Meany as president and Walter Reuther as vice-president of the federation and director of the new Industrial Union Department, one of its important early moves was to establish an Ethical Practices Committee, which formulated and applied a code of ethics, with the power to recommend expulsion of any national union found in violation. In 1957 the International Brotherhood of Teamsters was expelled from the federation on this basis. It has remained independent ever since.

THE POSTWAR PROBLEM OF WORK RULES

One of the most difficult problems for postwar collective bargaining involved the question of work rules in basic steel, in the railroad industry, and in longshoring on the West Coast.[13]

---

12   For a succinct account of the merger and its problems, see [1, pp. 58-61].

13   For balanced and perceptive discussions of this highly inflammatory topic, see [7, pp. 317-341]; [2, pp. 260-280]; and [3, pp. 23-72].

Perhaps it should be noted at the outset that work rules exhibit considerable variety and are found in one form or another throughout industry. Usually they have their origin not in cynical featherbedding or in attempts to compel a firm to hire unneeded workers, but in what seems to be a reasonable arrangement at the time, say, to fix safe limits on slingloads, to distinguish jobs and types of work, to keep the pace of work at a reasonable rate, or to prescribe the makeup of work crews [7, pp. 317-323]. Then, with the passage of time, the intrusion of new technology, and perhaps innovations in work organization and processes, the restrictions imposed by certain work rules do tend to compel the continued employment of excess labor. At this point the battle is likely to become joined between management and the union.

During the decade after 1955, the issue of work rules assumed an unusual degree of prominence in American industrial relations. The first major case involved the so-called local practices clause in steel, which had been negotiated originally in 1947 to preserve intact work practices then in effect [7, pp. 331-332]. Among other impacts, this clause operated to prevent the companies from reducing the sizes of production crews unless the change was associated with a clear-cut technological change. Some managements considered the clause extremely onerous because it froze crew sizes at what they considered to be the inflated levels of World War II, absent a justifying technological change, or because it compelled the introduction of uneconomic changes. In any case, the issue was raised by the employer spokesman in the 1959 negotiations, and proved to be so intractable that it was in large part responsible for a strike that lasted for 114 days—the longest in the history of the industry.

In the upshot, the length and bitterness of this strike led both parties to form "human relations" committees to study sources of conflict and to find ways to remove or reduce them. Even today both sides continue to share a concern for avoiding traumatic strikes of the sort that took place in 1959.

The second major episode involved the very intricate system of work rules in longshoring on the West Coast. This case differed from basic steel in several important respects. No strike ever took place during the period 1957-60 when the rules were at issue. More than this, it was the International Longshoremen's and Warehousemen's Union itself that raised the issue, simply because its leaders had been aware for years that the rules they had won through a coastwide strike in 1934 had always been restrictive and therefore costly, both in intent and in effect. Their goal from 1957 onward was to save jobs and wage incomes in an industry that was in long-run decline. Their problem was to find a way to relax these rules that would (1) cut costs and thus (2) conserve jobs, and yet (3) be acceptable to the membership and, of course, the employers.

The West Coast system of rules was probably the most thorough in American industry.[14] From its inception in 1934, the system was union

---

14   This account is based mainly on [3, pp. 25-72].

created and union oriented. Its central purposes were to make and protect jobs and to stabilize the earnings of the work force. As Hartman suggests, this was not a case that conformed to the principle of Slichter, Healy, and Livernash that work rules typically start from a reasonable basis such as safety, then become restrictive at a later time, when changes have affected the work process. On the contrary, the intent of the longshoring rules was restrictive from the outset, as the product of deep-seated grievances and of a union that required such rules to perform its basic functions for its members.

Summarized briefly, one group of rules was directed at control of the work force, through regulations of entry, control of the hiring hall and dispatcher, and control of assignments and discipline. Here the main objectives were a stabilized work force and equal division of the work opportunity.

The second group of rules concerned the work or production process, by means of such devices as minimum manning, maximum weights for slingloads, limits upon pace of work and effort per unit of time, and requirements for multiple handling of cargo to deny shippers the economies of packing containers or "prepalletizing" loads before their arrival at the dock.

Taken as a whole, these and many other special rules lowered productivity, raised costs, and reduced the tonnage available after the end of the Korean War. Then between 1956 and 1959, the employers and the union moved toward a new approach that can best be described as one in which the union "sold" most of its work rules to the employers, except where safety was involved, in exchange for a system of job and earnings security—at a cost of $29 million to the operators, extending over 1959-66. In essence, early retirement would be encouraged by special bonuses, while the remaining group of registered longshoremen would be guaranteed, regardless of available work load, average total weekly earnings of 35 hours times the current straight-time rate [3, p. 102.]. In exchange, all of the restrictive rules were lifted. The employers finally had regained control of the work process, and this enabled the industry to begin its recovery from the doldrums.

The last of the major postwar work rules cases was the most complex of all: that of the railroads. Because of the great age of the industry, some of its rules were very old, while others were imposed by the federal government when it operated the railroads during the latter part of World War I. Another complicating factor was the craft structure of unionism in the industry, such that even today there are 18 organizations—a situation that makes work-separation rules highly important. Finally, the postwar context of the industry was one of severe contraction of traffic and an intensive mechanization program to eliminate labor—factors that brought about very rapid attrition of the work force until very recently.

Beginning in the mid-1950s, the earnings of the industry began to slip alarmingly, a process that accelerated as the building of the interstate highway system caused diversion of much freight business to trucks.

In a desperate effort to obtain relief, management initiated a campaign of publicity whose central theme was "featherbedding" and whose targets were certain union practices, along with state legislation requiring "full crews" and train limits on freight trains.

In fact, the actual work rules problem was much bigger than this. Among its principal elements were—and largely remain today—the following.[15] (1) There is a "dual" basis of pay for road crews in which a full day's work is defined to be eight hours' service *or* completion of a 100-mile run for freight trains (12.5 miles per hour implied speed) or a 150-mile run for passenger service (25 miles per hour implied speed). If a freight crew can average 25 miles per hour, it can complete a full day in four hours, either ending its run at this point or earning overtime for all additional time worked. In short, management is confronted with an obsolete piece-rate system that inflates earnings relative to actual time worked. (2) Although some concessions have been made here, another problem concerns the separation of "over-the-road" from "yard" work, in which separate crews are required to do only switching, while road crews must be paid an extra day's pay if they perform switching as well as road duties. (3) Then there is the "crew consist" question, which boils down to how many employees in how many occupations (engineer, fireman, conductor, brakeman) are needed on a freight train. In a typical case today, a railroad can operate safely, in its judgment, with only an engineer, a conductor, and at most one brakeman. But the rule may call for two or more brakemen. (4) Intertwined with this dispute, which still continues, was the so-called fireman-off issue for freight runs not hauled by steam power.

After 20 years of effort, the carriers managed to obtain repeal of the restrictive state legislation and to create a bargaining issue over elimination of the fireman. However, it is a fair commentary upon the rigidity and unproductiveness of collective bargaining in the industry that it ultimately required an act of Congress to resolve the fireman-off issue—even after an offer was made very similar in principle to that in the West Coast longshoring settlement, to protect any employees actually displaced. As for the other issues, they still remain alive today, with "crew consist" the current target of the carriers' long battle to change the ancient rules of their industry.

At this point it is reasonable to ask why major union concessions were possible in the Pacific maritime industry, while collective bargaining failed almost completely on the railroads. The answer is probably two-fold: Given the craft structure of the railroad unions, complete resistance was the price

---

15   For a careful and extensive review, see [5].

for organizational survival. Beyond this, government regulation of and interference with labor-management relations on the railroads was so extensive and so rigid that it greatly reduced the incentives of both sides to engage in genuine bargaining. Indeed, government intervention has both created and perpetuated problems, instead of helping the parties to solve them.

SOME MAJOR POSTWAR INNOVATIONS IN COLLECTIVE BARGAINING

Over the past 30 years, a large shift has occurred in the composition of the labor-cost dollar—a shift that in good part has been a product of collective bargaining. Before World War II, a dollar of labor cost was accounted for overwhelmingly by straight-time pay for time actually worked. By 1972, however, straight-time pay costs throughout private nonagricultural industry were only 78.5 percent of total compensation, while 21.5 percent involved "fringe benefits," that is, employer contributions for overtime premiums or to pensions, health and welfare plans, and a host of other payments not directly connected with time worked, such as paid vacations and sick leave [9, p. 235].[16] As of 1975, a U.S. Chamber of Commerce survey of 761 companies mainly of large size showed that fringe benefits averaged 35.4 percent of payroll [4, pp. 43-44].

Looking first at private pension and retirement plans, it is estimated that for 1973, 33.1 million workers—just under half of those in the private nonagricultural sector—were participating in these plans, while annual contributions totalled $22.1 billion [8, pp. 16-17]. In 1972, private pension plans throughout industry accounted for 3.3 percent of payroll costs, while an additional 3.7 percent was paid into the social security system [9, p. 235].

The movement for private pension plans had its origin in voluntary efforts of employers to attract and to hold workers at the peak of the wartime scarcity. Initially, the unions were either opposed or indifferent. Then, after a decision in 1948 by the NLRB holding that these plans were a negotiable issue, organized labor seized the opportunity to gain a voice in the plans and to expand their benefits [8, pp. 33-35]. Thus, between 1950 and 1973 the number of active workers covered soared by 238 percent. By 1974, 78 percent of all plant workers throughout industry were covered by some type of retirement pension plan.[17]

---

16   If premium pay for overtime is included with straight time, remaining fringe benefits were 19.5 percent. These data reflect many small employers, whose fringe payments are low.

17   The Social Security Administration estimated recently that in 1974 coverage was 30 million persons, with about half under collectively bargained plans.

The other fringe benefit of major importance concerns health insurance and welfare plans—a development that the unions have pushed hard ever since the end of the war. As of 1972-74, the federal government estimates that over 90 percent of plant workers in all industry were covered by insurance plans for hospitalization, surgical, medical, and life, while 74 percent had catastrophe insurance and 83 percent had sickness and accident insurance and/or sick leave. Office workers had slightly higher proportions. Excluding legally required workmen's compensation payments, these employers contributed 3.7 percent of all compensation costs for these purposes [9, pp. 224, 235]. For the larger firms in the Chamber of Commerce survey, by constrast, 3.9 percent of payroll went for health insurance, 0.8 percent for life insurance premiums, and 0.5 percent for combined premiums—or a total of 5.2 percent of payroll [4, p. 45].

Before leaving the topic of bargaining innovations, brief attention must be paid to the setting of wage rates as such. In this field, WLB controls—in particular the "Little Steel" formula for 1942—provided the principle that wage rates should be raised to "catch up" with the price level, through a mechanism later known as COLA (for cost-of-living-adjustment). COLA devices spread once more with the Korean War, and again when inflation began its present long-term acceleration in 1966.

Finally, it was in the postwar period that "patterns" and "orbits of coercive comparison" became words of art in the economics of collective bargaining. In basic steel, a *de facto* form of industrywide bargaining was brought into being by the joint action of the United Steelworkers (USW) and the large employers. Here the union borrowed the notion of a prototype central bargain from its original parent, the United Mine Workers, and then extended it to other regions of its industrial domain, such as the mining of aluminum, iron ore, and nonferrous metals. Here was a "pattern of settlement" in one form.

The other version was the "pattern-following" technique chosen by the Automobile Workers. Here the procedure called for developing a model contract with a particular producer, carefully chosen in advance. Once agreement was reached, the model could then be demanded of the other employers in automobile production, and then extended *seriatim* to firms in aircraft and farm equipment manufacturing.

Pattern-following provides two advantages: It does not require a costly industrywide strike, and yet it can bring about uniform contracts by shrewd exploitation of the employers' sensitivity to changes in their market shares in industries in which sellers are few.

As an economic matter, both joint committee bargaining in steel and pattern-following in autos have a special attraction for employers in these industries: Both techniques tend to produce close uniformity in settlements, and this avoids disturbances in comparative labor costs per unit of product among the different producers and their plants. This is important wherever an industry is characterized by few sellers (oligopoly), because in such cases individual market shares are extremely sensitive to price changes by rivals. At the same time, the union avoids the internecine strife that would occur if increases in wages and benefits varied greatly among the different plants.

REFERENCES

1. Bloom, Gordon F., and Herbert R. Northrup. *Economics of Labor Relations.* 7th ed. Homewood, IL: Richard D. Irwin, 1973.

2. Bok, Derek C., and John T. Dunlop. *Labor and the American Community.* New York: Simon and Schuster, 1970.

3. Hartman, Paul T., *Collective Bargaining and Productivity: The Longshore Mechanization Agreement.* Berkeley and Los Angeles: University of California Press, 1969.

4. *Labor Relations Yearbook:* 1976. Washington, D.C. Bureau of National Affairs, 1977.

5. Presidential Railroad Commission. *Report of the Presidential Railroad Commission.* Washington, D.C.: Government Printing Office, February 1962.

6. Slichter, Sumner H. "The Taft-Hartley Act." *Quarterly Journal of Economics* 63, No. 1 (February 1949).

7. Slichter, Sumner H., James J. Healy, and E. Robert Livernash. *The Impact of Collective Bargaining on Management.* Washington, D.C.: The Brookings Institution, 1960.

8. Ture, Norman B. *The Future of Private Pension Plans.* Washington, D.C.: American Enterprise Institute for Public Policy Research, 1976.

9. U.S. Department of Labor, Bureau of Labor Statistics. *Handbook of Labor Statistics 1977.* Bulletin 1966. Washington, D.C.: Government Printing Office, 1977.

Some Structural   4
and Organizational
Aspects of
American Unionism

This chapter will look briefly at the structure and organization of the contemporary labor movement and will also examine briefly the process of collective bargaining itself.

The easiest method to acquire a grasp of the structure of unionism is to start with the basic cellular units and then to move upward in order of increasing complexity. Because even in its own view the AFL-CIO regards unionism essentially as a system of bargaining institutions, and also because the basic law of labor relations is inextricably intertwined with these institutions, it is convenient to start with the notion of the bargaining unit.

THE BARGAINING UNIT AND THE BARGAINING PROCESS

The bargaining unit consists of a group of jobs and the people who work on those jobs. Accordingly, it is a piece of job territory whose employees are exclusively represented by a union in all matters concerning bargaining over wages, hours, and other conditions of work. In turn this territory and its incumbents are governed by the terms of a collective agreement or contract achieved through bargaining, and embodying the rights and obligations of the employer, the union, and the employees as regards the employment relationship.

Some bargaining units have a history as old as the original AFL. Many others have been created through "certification" by the NLRB or through voluntary private agreements consistent with applicable law. If the unit has been established through certification, then it is the product of an initial representation election conducted by the board. In these instances the unit has its origin as a "voting district" whose boundaries have been defined by the board. Then, if a particular union is the winner of that election, it thereby acquires the status of exclusive bargaining representative for the unit and its employees.[1] In some situations, the parties (the union and the employer) by mutual consent may combine these units for bargaining purposes, as a matter of joint convenience. Without such consent, the voting district leads directly to a bargaining unit of identical characteristics.

In strict interpretation, the concept of exclusive representation provides for a system of collective bargaining that excludes any rival union from participation for the duration of the agreement, save for this exception: during the 30 days prior to the expiration of the agreement, a rival organization can raise "a question concerning representation" if it can show the board that at least 30 percent of the unit employees wish to have a new election.

Thus the consequence of exclusive representation is that it confers a temporary grant of monopoly power for the life of the contract, a grant that typically becomes permanent through endless renewals. The monopoly itself is peculiar in kind, perhaps best described as an open-ended cartel of employees who act through a union as their agent for negotiating and also administering the agreement.[2] In this peculiar arrangement, the union itself has nothing to sell and nothing to deliver to the employer on its own part, because the labor services involved are actually provided by the individual employees, and they cannot be compelled to work if they choose not to do so. Thus what the union actually does is to act as the agent of the unit employees, to seek agreement with the employer about the terms and conditions under which these employees as a group will consent to work for the life of that agreement.

Under the law, both the employer and the employee are forbidden to depart from these terms, for example, by side agreements involving particular employees. More than this, the law requires the employer to conduct all relevant dealings with unit employees through their union, not behind its back. At the same time, of course, the employer retains whatever managerial discretion the contract accords him or her.

There are numerous varieties of bargaining units. Among the principal ones are the following: (1) The single plantwide unit is typically a "production and maintenance" (blue-collar) workers' unit, sometimes also including nonsupervisorial white-collar employees. Such units are very common in manufacturing and usually involve the old CIO unions. (2) By contrast there is the unit that is a segment of a multiunit bargaining structure. Many variants of these have developed: a craft unit carved out of a production-worker group in a manufacturing plant; a complex of craft units in a newspaper plant or a copper-mining and smelting complex; or a complex of

---

1   The union must obtain a majority of eligible votes actually cast, where one of the options is "no union." If no competing option yields more than a plurality, the board will hold a runoff election between the top two.

2   "Open-ended" because new employees may be added to the unit.

operating, back shop, and clerical units on a large railroad system. (3) Next, there is the formal multiplant unit, or what amounts to the same thing, an informal coalition of plant units acting together to coordinate their bargaining, say, for example, as in the automobile industry. (4) Finally, there exists the multiemployer unit that bargains with an association of employers also acting as a formal group, as with the San Francisco Employers' Council or the Pacific Maritime Association. Within manufacturing, single-employer units are most common, while multiemployer units are rare except in the apparel and food industries. In contrast, within nonmanufacturing, association bargaining is very common, as in trucking, construction, and the railroad industry.

At this point it should be noted that a bargaining unit and a negotiating unit need not always be the same thing, as some of the variants just considered readily indicate. Put differently, situations occur in which it is to the mutual convenience of both sides to enlarge the ambit of negotiations beyond the bounds of the formal scope of the bargaining unit as it originally came to be defined. This is a matter of some complexity. Where competing employers are few in number (oligopoly), the sensitivity of their market shares to each other's pricing actions will encourage them to create a formal association, to act together informally through a committee, or to engage in pattern-following—all in the service of avoiding serious divergences in contractually negotiated labor costs. Where competing employers are large in number, they will have strong incentive to create an association, bargaining for a single agreement to prevent being whipsawed and to assure some effectiveness if a strike should occur. In all of these situations, the union gains a considerable measure of uniformity in wages and working conditions, which is an important advantage for preserving internal political cohesion.[3]

Many unionized employers actually fit into none of these categories of bargaining systems. Where such is the case, the tendency is to follow patterns of increase influenced by what the union has won elsewhere and by wage behavior in the labor market from which they draw their employees.

At this point we should say a little about the process of collective bargaining. There is rather broad agreement that unions usually achieve a wage premium averaging 15 percent over nonunion employees generally, that they establish this advantage early in their bargaining relationship with the employer or employers, and that their main objective regarding basic wage rates is to preserve this advantage indefinitely thereafter.

In addition to this primary wage objective, the union usually demands a security clause to protect its ranks from encroachment by nonmember employees. In industrial or factory unions, the solution is a union shop. In

---

3 The geographic scope of these negotiating units and systems is strongly influenced by the scope of competition in the product market. Automobiles involve a national if not an international market, while construction has a local and regional scope.

those unions whose members tend to work on short tenure with any one employer—as with many employees in printing or construction—the traditional solution has been the closed shop. Although the closed shop was outlawed by the Taft-Hartley Act, it has survived *de facto* through control of the hiring hall and its referrals, through special arrangements in which the employer agrees "to prefer" workers with lengthy seniority in the trade.

Once its wage advantage and its security have been established, the union can concentrate upon a series of more diverse objectives as each negotiation rolls around. These would include the whole panoply of fringe benefits; changes in job rate differentials; stronger seniority (length of service) provisions for layoffs, recalls, and transfers where industrial unionism is involved; and rectification of a wide variety of complaints, from emergency call-outs on Sunday to five more minutes for daily washup time.

Before leaving the subject of bargaining we should consider the employer side as well, although traditionally employers have been less likely to initiate demands than to resist those of the union.

At the heart of the typical employer's bargaining position is a desire to protect the right to manage the firm. Typically this leads to insistence upon a "management rights" clause and to avoiding as far as possible concessions through other provisions that would unduly restrict freedom of assignments: decisions about manning and machine speeds; introduction of new equipment, processes, and forms of work organization; or contracting out of certain functions or services (maintenance and repair, cafeterias, etc.).

So much for bargaining and bargaining units. The next step is to examine the structure of unionism itself, beginning with the smallest unit extant, the local, of which there exist over 70,000 in almost bewildering diversity.[4]

THE UNION LOCAL

The locals can be viewed as the building blocks of the national unions, although some of them are quite independent of any such affiliation or are associated directly with the AFL-CIO. For those that are tied to national unions, some are older than the national body, as in the Plumbers' case, while others were organized from above, as in much of the United Steelworkers. In good part, the difference rests upon the contrasting histories of the AFL—originally mainly a craft-minded organization—and the CIO, which was created deliberately to organize industrial workers according to product lines and groups.

Before we look into the organization and functioning of locals, it is desirable to attempt to distinguish them as to types. One principal variant is

---

4   In addition to Estey [4], I have relied upon Leonard R. Sayles and George Strauss [5], Jack Barbash [1, pp. 26-54], and Neil W. Chamberlain and James W. Kuhn [2, pp. 191-203].

the craft or occupational local, such as is found in the building and printing trades, and in the hotel and restaurant industry. Such locals deal with many employers in the trade. In turn they are affiliated with the local building or printing trades council, with the latter as an intermediary body or permanent coalition of craft locals whose functions include joint collective bargaining and the promotion of various political interests.

At the same time, the craft local holds a charter from the national union with which it is affiliated. In turn, the national may have constitutional power to approve strikes or the payment of strike benefits by the local. However, if the product market for the trade represented by the local is local, as in construction, newspapers, or restaurants, then negotiations will be conducted by the local. In such situations, the national union may still have important functions of its own, but for practical purposes the local *is* the union.

A second variant is the local in factory unionism. In large plants, the local is limited to a single plant—for example, Local 600 of the United Auto Workers at the Ford River Rouge plant has some 40,000 members. However, in other cases an industrial local may embrace several small plants or competing employers. In either form, if the product market for these plants is national or international, then the national union will keep tight control over negotiations in an attempt to "take wages out of competition" by striving for uniform contracts. At the same time, the local will still play a role, mainly by conducting negotiations concerned with local issues at the plant level.

Perhaps a tentative rule may be suggested as follows: Where bargaining involving factory unionism concerns local markets and single-plant contracts, the local is likely to command more membership interest and participation. In other words, interest tends to decrease as the geographic reach of the market increases, while the role of the national officers and their technical advisors tends to increase for the same reason.

Mention should also be made of a third and final form of union local, sometimes called the "amalgamated" type. In effect, this type of local has a large membership, embraces different industries and occupations, deals with diverse product markets, and of course negotiates with many employers. Examples of such locals are found in the Teamsters and the Retail and Wholesale Workers in large metropolitan areas. Such locals are primarily catchall organizations set up for administrative purposes. The typical union member's interest and concern will lie with the segment or division containing his or her particular industry or trade.

Turning next to the governance of local unions, we start with a constitution and a set of officers that includes a president, a vice-president, a secretary, and a treasurer. Depending upon the kind of local, there will be provided an executive board, a negotiating committee, and a grievance committee. Finally, there will probably also exist, particularly in factory unions, a group of elected shop stewards, whose duties are to deal with grievances in the first instance, to resolve small controversies, to build support for the union, and to help in the formulation and negotiation of contract demands.

For locals of the craft type, the key official is the business agent. His or her tasks are diverse: to police the agreement with employers, to protect the union's job territory from infringements or raiding, to get jobs for members, and to settle disputes among contending factions. As a full-time officer, the business agent becomes involved in negotiations and speaks for his or her organization in bargaining coalitions with other crafts in local building trades councils.

With factory unionism, the situation is somewhat different at the local level. The regular officers are usually full-time employees paid by the employer and in a sense likely to be restrained by this dependence. Also, it is quite typical for the national union to provide several business agents or "international representatives" to aid the various locals in negotiations, in the higher stages of grievance procedure, and in arbitration proceedings. Typically, these representatives are appointed and paid by the national, and thus they function independently of the local. As a general rule, the business agent is the most important local official in organized labor, regardless of the type of union.

Discussion of the politics of local unionism invariably brings up comments about "apathy" and "minority control," along with other observations about union democracy or the lack of it.

"Apathy" is a term often used to describe members' attitudes toward routine meetings of local unions. Indeed, this complaint is often heard from union leaders themselves, and it holds some truth. Ordinary American union members support their organizations in the decisive sense, and when the issue is right, for example, a bitter dispute or a strike, they will do so with passion. But at other times they tend to regard their union cards as a form of insurance, and they are likely to avoid routine meetings.

In the upshot, then, the standards of conduct for the union local tend to be influenced by the minority that regularly turns up at the meetings. Who are they? For the most part this group is a blend of idealists, activists of various sorts, the politically ambitious, and some loyal stalwarts who look upon attendance as a duty not to be shirked lightly. In turn, the relative weighting of this mixture determines the quality of the meetings and through them the general repute of the local. But here the role of the business agent must not be overlooked, for in a sense he or she serves as a mediator between the local and the employers.

The quality of an employer's relationship with a local can run all the way from excellent to bad. Normally it will be reasonably good or at least mutually acceptable, particularly where it has extended over a lengthy period. It has often been remarked that an employer "gets the kind of union he deserves." If he detests the very principle of collective bargaining, or the business agent with whom he must deal, union-management relations will not prosper. On the contrary, if the employer understands unionism and its needs, and accepts it tacitly as a permanent institution, typically the two sides will establish a permanent accommodation.

Thus, while it is true that in one respect their relationship is an adversary one simply because the employer is inevitably concerned with costs, sales, and profit, while the union is politically committed to higher wages and improved benefits and working conditions, in the broader and long run sense the survival of both sides depends upon their mutual recognition of each other's needs and interests. In this way conflict tends to be over-shadowed by cooperation as the representatives of both sides acquire experience and sophistication in continued dealings with each other. Indeed, many employers would concede at least privately that the union is of value in some respects. It is a means of learning about grievances, plant morale, and the quality of supervision. Perhaps most important of all, through collective bargaining American employers have acquired a kind of social contract in which they have gained the stability of long-term agreements and a no-strike clause for the duration of the agreement. In exchange, they have conceded to the union the system of voluntary grievance arbitration and have ruled out the wildcat (unauthorized and illegal) strike. In consequence, the employers have gained the benefits of uninterrupted production together with a valuable device for exposing problems in administration of the plant.

THE NATIONAL UNION

Sometimes termed "internationals" because their charters include Canada or Puerto Rico, the national unions long since have become the real center of power in American unionism after they first began to be formed in the 1820s. The reasons are basic. The national holds the charter granted by the federation, through which exclusive title to organizing territory is conferred. Except for negotiation of local conditions or for decentralized industries such as construction, the nationals control collective bargaining in their industry or trade. This of course places them in the central role in the American labor movement because that movement is so thoroughly domi-nated by bargaining activity. Furthermore, the nationals—not the AFL-CIO—have the members, and through this, the dues revenue that in part supports the federation (the "per cap," for *per capita* charge, as it is known), and in whole provides the basic income of the movement. And finally, it is the national union that decides upon negotiating demands and strategy and strike policy, except where product markets are mainly local and decen-tralization has been feasible. As the cases of the Mine Workers and the Teamsters have shown over the years, a strong national union can survive without difficulty as an independent body outside of the AFL-CIO. But the federation conceivably could not possibly survive without its member national unions.

At this point, one may ask, Why have locals at all? In general, all locals serve as a necessary and convenient point of contact with the members, for collecting dues, for formulating and communicating national policy, and for conducting relations with employers. In turn, the national may coordinate and enforce negotiating policies, pay strike benefits, represent the membership in national political affairs, and undertake organizing campaigns.

As we noted earlier, in the very early years the locals were supreme and there were no national unions. Although some nationals were formed in the 1820s and 1830s, all of them became extinct with the depression of 1837. But the impulse to bring the locals together in appropriate national unions did not die, as developments after 1850 were to show. In 1974 there were 175 national unions and 37 employee associations. Most of them have been built "from the ground up" by fusion of the locals, although those originating with the CIO were formed first and then organized "downward" to build their locals.

The central reason for the national union is economic: As transportation improved, product markets widened, and locals in a given craft, trade, or industry were forced into competition with each other as employers attempted to meet lower prices of new rivals by cutting wages and lowering working standards.[5]

Economic factors are still the basic reason for the nationals, because modern transportation has broadened more and more product markets to national or even international scope. Put in another way, the triumph of national unionism reflects the continuing dominating importance of the technique of collective bargaining in the American labor movement and the continuing weakness of alternative political objectives. Political action, of course, is much more important today than it was in 1886 or even in 1945. But it has still to become a substitute for bargaining, while on its own terms its aims tend to be specific and relatively short-run, in sharp distinction from the far more ambitious goal of control over the means of production, as illustrated by the socialist tradition of Europe.

In its relations with its locals, the national provides both regulatory and supportive functions. On the regulatory side it usually can require its approval of negotiating demands, strike action, and contractual settlements, and it also has a voice in local finances. In the extreme, it can place a local in trusteeship, subject now to the requirements of the Landrum-Griffin law. Then, on the services side, the national provides the locals with counsel about negotiating and strike strategy and expertise regarding technical matters such as pensions and health and welfare plans. Finally, the national

---

5   In some of the construction trades, the force making for formation of nationals was a little different: the problem of the "traveling member" who could undercut local wages or serve as a strikebreaker. Through the national the issuance of membership cards could be controlled and standards enforced.

has the strike fund, which gives it, through its control over benefits, additional leverage of considerable power over policies of the locals.

From the standpoint of governance, the national sets its objectives and major policies through a convention composed of delegates from the locals, theoretically allocated in proportion to local memberships. The convention, in turn, chooses the president and an executive board. Between conventions, the president runs the union in the overall sense, although the business agents play the critical role in employer relations and negotiations. In many cases, however, the national president will exert much influence over the selection of staff, office personnel, regional officers, and business agents.

In 1886, as we have seen, the autonomous national union with its own exclusive jurisdiction constituted the fundamental building block of the old AFL, while the latter was a weak and dependent organization created largely for the defense of craft union interests against possible raids by the Knights of Labor and the advocates of various socialist programs. In the ensuing 90 years, the nationals are still the dominant bodies; indeed, with the no-raiding pact of 1953 and the AFL-CIO merger two years later, there has occurred a substantial restoration of the original principle of exclusive jurisdiction, except for occasional invasions by the independent Teamsters, who can be described as the rogue elephant of today's American labor movement. Meanwhile, collective bargaining has continued to occupy the commanding position in American unionism, except that today the industrial unions now enjoy the greater prominence while the crafts have lost much of their power or have largely turned themselves into industrial unions to stay alive and effective. At the same time, the AFL-CIO is a much stronger and much more influential body than the original AFL ever was.

THE FEDERATION

The AFL-CIO is both a creature of its member national unions and a large organization with officials, a staff, and a bureaucracy of its own. It issues jurisdictional charters to some of its member unions, although in most cases these long antedate the new federation. In turn the member unions pay a monthly per capita tax based upon membership (about 50 cents per member per month plus special levies) to the federation, and these payments constitute the principal revenues of the latter body. However, it should be emphasized that the federation as such does no collective bargaining and has no employee members. It is in essence a peak association created for other purposes.

Put succinctly, the federation is the official public advocate of the interests of organized labor in various areas of national life. But since those interests are still so largely market oriented and therefore are expressed through collective bargaining, the federation leaves the actual negotiating to the national unions, while confining itself to an active involvement with legislation that affects their bargaining strength. In this capacity, the principal concern of the federation is with political influence and action at the national level. Through its Committee on Political Education (COPE) it endorses candidates, provides campaign contributions, and mobilizes union members for help to candidates and for voter-registration drives. In addition, the AFL-CIO engages in a substantial amount of lobbying with Congress and the executive branch in support of or in opposition to measures of interest to it. Through its first and only president so far, George Meany, the federation has had direct personal access to every president of the United States from Eisenhower to Carter. Beyond this, Meany and his colleagues on the executive council (who are themselves mostly presidents of national unions) also have had close contacts with cabinet officers heading federal departments or agencies of particular interest to them.

For a labor movement as strongly committed to collective bargaining as the American one, it is hardly surprising that the politics of the AFL-CIO are so largely oriented to bargaining interests rather than issues of broader scope. Put in a more academic way, ever since 1886 its politics have been pragmatic and short-run. They involve what Max Weber termed an "ethic of immediate ends," rather than those programs of social reconstruction that he described as an "ethic of ultimate ends."

Consider a few examples. The AFL-CIO supports big spending programs, income redistribution through steeper progressive taxation, and higher minimum wages because of a deep conviction that these measures increase employment and income, and thereby increase the ability of unions to win gains in wages and fringe benefits. These and related programs might well be called the "macroeconomic policy of organized labor."

On the "microeconomic" side, the federation has pressed strongly for legislation to permit "common situs" picketing and to effect certain changes involving the NLRB. Regarding common situs, most building projects involve several specialized contractors and their unions, such as sheet metal and plumbing firms, and respectively, the Sheet Metal Workers and the Plumbers. Or the issue may involve an attempt to put presure on a nonunion contractor to compel his employees to join a union. Under the present restraints,[6] if the Plumbers get into a dispute with a contractor, they cannot picket the entire job, and in turn the members of their sister unions cannot legally refuse to cross such lines because they have no dispute with their own employers. After undergoing substantial losses of organized territory to nonunion

---

6   These restraints originated in the Taft-Hartley and Landrum-Griffin provisions restricting secondary boycotts, along with a decision of the Supreme Court in *NLRB v. Denver Building and Construction Trades Council* in 1951.

The issue involves a secondary boycott because the union in the dispute attempts by picketing to induce employees of third-party employers to refuse to work, to increase pressure on the employer directly involved in the dispute.

employers in home building and now in commercial and industrial construction, the building trades hope to regain some of their market power by repeal of the common situs restriction. In consequence this has now become a primary political objective of the federation.

Also on the microeconomic side, the federation strongly supported the proposed labor reform bill of 1977 (H.R. 8410), because it viewed its provisions as aiding the efforts of unions to organize nonunion employees and companies, with ensuing benefit to their market strength. This measure would have speeded up representation elections conducted by the NLRB to a minimum period of 15 days after filing a petition for an election. It would have required employers to allow union organizers opportunity to address the employees on the premises or during working time, if the employer had used the same privilege. Also, it would have penalized an employer for delaying recognition of a union after it had won a certification election—by awarding back pay for the difference in the employees' wages and the average gain elsewhere in the industry during the period of delay. And finally, the measure would have imposed "debarment" (denial) of federal contracts to an employer found in willful violation of NLRB orders [3]. However, Congress has tabled the measure and its prospects are very dubious now.

Leaving the issue of politics at this point, we turn now to the organization of the federation. The ultimate source of power and policy is the biennial convention. Here the only two paid officers, the president and the secretary-treasurer, are elected and enabling motions and declarative resolutions are voted on. Most of the delegates come from member unions and are apportioned by relative per capita taxes, meaning that representation is weighted by membership.

Between conventions, the executive council, and a subordinate body called the executive committee, supply leadership and management to the federation. In addition there is a staff group to deal with special functions such as research and international affairs.

Then there are the departments within the organization, for example, the Building and Construction Trades Department, the Industrial Union Department (IUD), the Union Label and Service Trades Department, the Metal Trades Department, the Railway Employees Department, the Maritime Trade Department Employees, and the Public Employees Department. Originally, the departments first began to appear with the building trades in the old AFL in 1908 as a means for bringing the craft unions in that industry together to consider common problems and interests—in essence a technique for resolving the problems of fragmentation inherent in all craft unionism. In the years since, new departments have been created for special purposes—for example, the IUD to foster Reuther's organizing goals, or the ULTS to promote the sale of union-made goods (and to encourage boycotts of nonunion products).

Two other subordinate bodies are the state labor councils and the city central labor councils. As their titles imply, both are concerned with joint union interests at the smaller geographic levels, where each body serves as spokesman for the common interests of its affiliated national unions and their locals. Except in rare cases such as the San Francisco general strike in 1934, the work of these bodies goes largely unnoticed by the general public.

This concludes our review of the structure and organization of American unionism, except for the question of the independent national unions. Apart from their lack of affiliation with the federation and its state and local bodies, these organizations are similar in all main respects to the national unions of the AFL-CIO. They include the country's two largest national bodies, the Teamsters (1,973,000 members) and the United Automobile Workers (1,545,000 members), as well as the United Mine Workers (220,000 members), the United Electrical Workers (163,000 members), the International Longshoremen's and Warehousemen's Union (45,000 members), and the old and once very prominent Brotherhood of Locomotive Engineers (less than 100,000 members) [6; all data for 1974]. Each of these unions goes its own way, for there is little of common interest ever likely to bring them together in a federation of their own.

However, there is one minor exception to this generalization: the rather close informal local relations between the building trades of the AFL-CIO and the Teamsters. The explanation lies in the strategic position of the Teamsters in delivery of construction materials and products, a position that makes it desirable to have a friendly association with them at the local level, regardless of the findings of the Ethical Practices Committee regarding the Teamsters' national leadership.

REFERENCES

1. Barbash, Jack, *American Unions: Structure, Government and Politics.* New York: Random House, 1967.

2. Chamberlain, Neil W., and James W. Kuhn. *Collective Bargaining.* 2d ed. New York: McGraw-Hill, 1965.

3. *Daily Labor Report.* No. 190 (Sept. 29, 1977).

4. Estey, Martin. *The Unions: Structure, Development, and Management.* 2d ed. New York: Harcourt, Brace, Jovanovich, 1976.

5. Sayles, Leonard R., and George Strauss. *The Local Union: Its Place in the Industrial Plant.* New York: Harper, 1953.

6. U.S. Department of Labor, Bureau of Labor Statistics. *Directory of National Unions and Employee Associations, 1975.* Bulletin 1937. Washington, D.C.: Government Printing Office, 1977.

Some 5
Economic
Impacts
of Unionism

Our review of the history and structure of American unionism leads naturally to a series of new questions to be considered in this chapter. Do unions really make any difference in wages? If, in fact, they can raise wages, how do they do it? And granting that they can raise them, are all unions equally effective or are some stronger than others? If such differences exist, what are the sources of the wage advantage of the more powerful organizations? And finally, what is the connection, if any, between unionism and inflation?

WAGES AT THE MICROECONOMIC LEVEL

The Initial Impact of the Union

Suppose that we start with a local labor market that is purely competitive and hence has large numbers of employers competing for the services of a larger number of workers who are identical in skill and efficiency. Because there is no union at the outset, the wage rate would be determined as shown in Fig. 5.1.[1]

At the point P, demand quantity and supply quantity, and, for that matter, demand price and supply price, are all equal. Thus the market can be said to be cleared: Any worker who wants to work at wage OW_0 can find a job at that wage, and any employer who is willing to pay the wage W_0 can get all the workers he wants.

---

1   This aggregate industry demand curve for labor is assumed here to have been corrected for any changes in the price of the product induced by (1) a change in the wage, and through this (2) a change in the product supply curve and price.

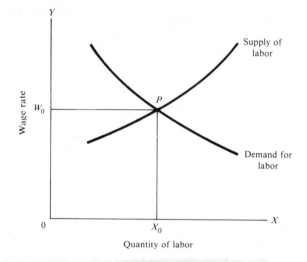

Fig. 5.1   Labor demand and supply under pure competition.

In this situation, the demand for labor is a composite obtained by adding the amounts of labor wanted by each of the firms at each possible wage, adjusting also for the derived changes in the price of the product and therefore in the marginal revenue product of each firm. In turn, each firm considered alone will have its own labor demand curve, which also will tilt downward to the right.[2] Figure 5.2 illustrates the position of a single firm at the market equilibrium wage, OW_0. Note that the quantity scale, OX, must be adjusted because the output of this firm is very small relative to the whole market.

More important, at the level of the firm the supply of labor is horizontal or infinitely elastic, irrespective of the quantity of labor taken by the firm. This means that the individual employer cannot influence the wage, whatever the amount of labor he or she may decide to use. Observe also the point P in Fig. 5.2: Here the marginal value product of labor equals the wage. Thus, by employing OX_0 labor, the employer has maximized returns from the use of this class of workers.

---

2   For the short run, the reason for this negative slope is the decline of marginal physical productivity following its initial increase. For pure competition, the price of the firm's product, P_a, will be constant. Accordingly, $MPP_1 \times P = MVP_1$; thus the firm's labor demand curve is a curve of the marginal value productivity of labor. For all cases in which the product demand curve of the firm has a negative slope, its marginal revenue cruve will lie below it; thus the firm's demand for labor will now be tilted further because both MPP_1 and MRA_a are falling.

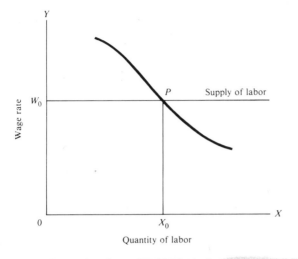

Fig. 5.2 Labor demand and supply to a single firm under pure competition.

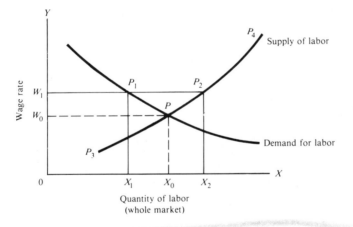

Fig. 5.3 Initial marketwide effects of a union-negotiated wage increase for the whole industry.

With this simple apparatus in hand, we can now tackle the main problem: the initial impact of the union upon organizing the industry. Its objective will be to negotiate a wage rate higher than OW_0. If it succeeds, OW_0 moves upward to OW_1 for all firms, as shown in Fig. 5.3.

Observe, now, that neither the demand or supply curve has moved its position. It follows then that W_0 is still the equilibrium wage that alone can clear the market. But since the union has now imposed a higher wage, W_1, the quantity of labor demanded, OX_1, falls short of the amount freely offered, OX_2. The reason for this involuntary unemployment, $X_2 - X_1$, is two-fold: (1) The union has imposed a higher wage than full competition would have allowed; this attracts additional labor, $X_2 - X_0$. (2) The employers reduce the quantity they are willing to take of this grade of labor because their goal is to maximize profits, and to accomplish this they must raise MVP_L until the condition is satisfied, $MVP_L = W$. Thus they reduce hiring to X_1 labor when the wage becomes W_1. Note also in passing that the union has succeeded in substituting a new market supply curve for labor, $W_1P_1P_2$, for the original supply curve indicated by P_3PP_2. It achieves this through the newly negotiated wage, which under law cannot be reduced for the duration of the contract without the union's consent. Between P_2 and P_4, of course, the old "free-market" supply curve continues to prevail.

As we noted in an earlier chapter, unionism on average tends initially to achieve a wage advantage of about 15 percent over comparable nonunion labor. Thereafter it preserves this advantage, trading off further gains in wages to acquire improvements in fringe benefits and working conditions. But in establishing this initial wage advantage, the union creates unemployment among firms affected. What happens to these unemployed workers?

Fig. 5.4 illustrates the case in which the unemployed workers flow from the unionized labor market into the nonunionized one. The principal impact is unemployment in Industry A after the union has forced up the wage to W_1. The excess labor, $X_2 - X_1$, now migrates to the nonunion sector represented here by Industry B. Outward migration from Industry A shifts its supply

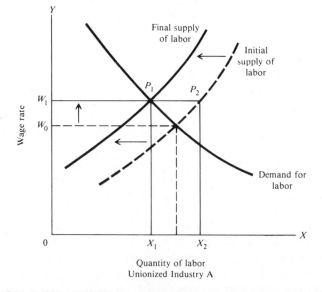

Fig. 5.4 Cross-effect of higher wage imposed by union on Industry A: Excess supply of unemployed labor, $X_2 - X_1$, migrates to Industry B, shifting its labor supply curve outward and reducing its wage to W_1.

curve *inward* until no involuntary unemployment remains in that sector. However, this same migration shows up as an *outward* movement of the labor supply curve in *B*, while the competition of these new workers for jobs pushes the nonunion wage down to W_1. Note that the average *slopes* of labor demand in *A* and *B* respectively will influence both the number of displaced workers migrating from *A* and the degree of decline of the wage in the competitive industry, *B*.

We can take this transfer process a step further by asking, What happens if some of those made unemployed in *A* choose to stay in that industry in hopes of becoming reemployed and if some workers in *B* become attracted to *A* because wages fall in *B* after having risen in *A*? Figure 5.5 indicates this situation.

In this case, some of the displaced workers prefer to remain in Industry *A* in hopes of eventual recall or of finding new jobs, while some workers *already* employed in Industry *B* become attracted to *A* because wages have risen there while falling in *B*. In result the net inward shift of the labor supply curve is reduced in *A* because of both influences. Thus the solid-line supply curve passing through *P* prevails, instead of the broken-line curve passing through P_1 in Industry *A*. The converse effect in Industry *B* is shown by the relationship of the solid-and-broken-line supply curve there.

What has happened is that a *queue* of unemployed has formed in Industry *A*, shown as $X_2 - X_1$, composed of workers in both sectors who believe their chances of getting a higher-paying job in *A* are preferable to

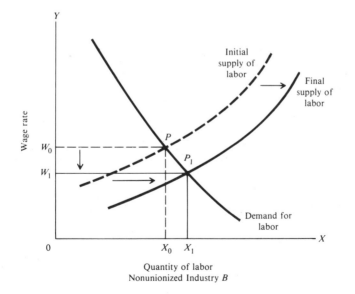

Fig. 5.4 *(continued)*

working at lower wages in B, even if there is a period of unemployment while waiting. Thus wages do not fall as much in B because net migration is reduced, while wages can not fall at all in A to absorb the involuntarily unemployed almost at once.[3]

In this instance, then, it is the queueing for jobs in the union sector that perpetrates the unemployment.

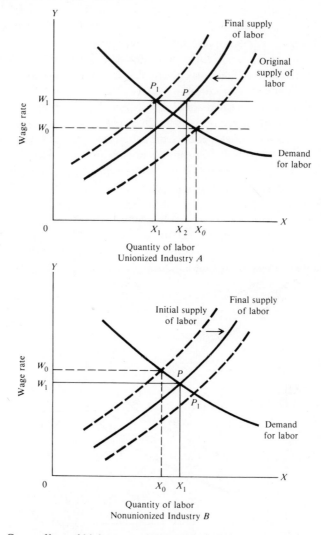

Fig. 5.5 Cross-effect of higher wage imposed in Industry A where outward migration is reduced in Industry A and induced in Industry B.

---

3   This model is used to explain why farm workers in underdeveloped countries migrate in large numbers to the cities to get better-paying jobs in industry, even when they know that the probability of unemployment is very high in the cities.

Before leaving this topic, the "correction" of the derived industry demand curve for labor mentioned in connection with Fig. 5.1 should be clarified. The problem concerns the effect of the higher wage upon the supply curve for the product of the industry. Figure 5.6 depicts the three main possibilities. In each instance, the same wage increase, by raising costs to the industry, has raised the supply curves uniformly, as shown by the broken lines. In case (a), there is no increase in price, and the whole burden of the wage increase is borne by reduced output from X_0 to X_1. In (b), there is no decrease in output, and the whole burden of the higher wage is reflected in the increase of price from P_0 to P_1. In (c), because the demand curve is negatively sloped but not vertical, the burden is shared: Price rises from P_0 to P_1, which is a lesser increase than in case (b), while output falls from X_0 to X_1, which is less than in case (a).

Since there is no product price change in (a), the derived industry demand curve for labor remains stable, because it is a curve reflecting the marginal value productivity of labor: $MVP_L = MPP_L \times P$. Marginal physical productivity of labor (MPP_L) is unchanged, while the price of the product of the industry, P, is also unchanged. The industry simply reduces production by laying workers off until MVP_L rises to equal the higher wage rate. In case (b), however, which is equally unrealistic, product price P does increase, to P_1. Thus the labor demand curve based upon MVP_L shifts upward and outward because product price has increased although MPP_L is unchanged. In this case there is no loss of sales, no loss of output, and the upshift in the industry labor demand curve is just sufficient to prevent any unemployment of labor.

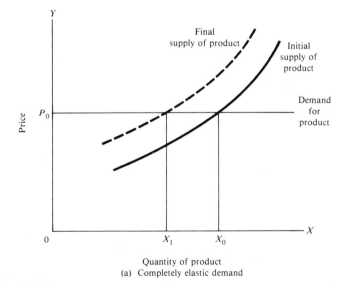

(a) Completely elastic demand

Fig. 5.6 Changes in price of industry product associated with uniform wage increase to the industry.

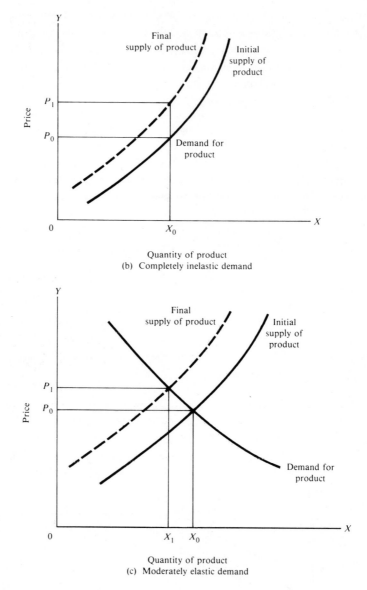

Quantity of product
(b) Completely inelastic demand

Quantity of product
(c) Moderately elastic demand

Fig. 5.6   *(continued)*

But in between these extremes lies the practical case. Here, too, the price rises, but not as much as in (b); further, output falls, but not as much as in (a). Thus the industry demand curve for labor, which is based upon $MPP_L \times P$, shifts upward and outward with the rise in P to P_1, but not as much as in (b). This "corrected" demand curve will yield less unemployment than the original one in (a), which presumes product price is unchanged.

To sum up, then, for all practical cases unemployment will follow the wage increase as employers cut back on labor input to achieve $MVP_L = W_1$. But the amount of unemployment will vary inversely with the steepness of the slope of the demand curve for the product of the industry, as Fig. 5.6 shows. Finally, then, in all cases except (a), the initial wage increase induces a partially offsetting upshift in the labor demand curve, rather than a simple move upward along the "uncorrected" demand curve.

The Elasticity of Demand for Labor

This is a convenient point at which to look more carefully at the notion of elasticity. In essence, elasticity measures the responsiveness of a change in quantity associated with a given change of price. The most common form of the concept is *point elasticity,* which is a ratio of the following form:

$$\text{Elasticity} \quad \frac{\text{Percentage change in quantity}}{\text{Percentage change in wage rate}}$$

It can be applied to both the demand for and supply of a given type of labor, starting with any pair that links a wage rate to an associated quantity of labor, usually in man-hours, and following with a small change in the wage and the new quantity associated with the new wage.[4] Referring to Fig. 5.6, case (a) yields an infinite elasticity of demand at any point, case (b) is zero-elastic for demand at any point, while case (c) has various point elasticities of demand along the entire curve.

For the problems to follow, we can employ the simpler and more useful concept of *absolute elasticity,* which measures the slopes of labor demand and supply curves, and which relates the absolute change of quantity brought about by a given unit change in price [1, pp. 121-124, for a fuller discussion]. Thus in Fig. 5.7 we have two demand curves for labor, plus a "unit" or standardized change in the wage rate common to both cases. *PA* is an *inelastic* labor demand curve and *PB* an *elastic* one, because the same wage increase, *QP*, causes a fall in employment of only *RQ* in the first case, as against *SQ* in the second.[5] It is this difference in response of respective quantities, which depends upon the *slopes* of the demand curves, that has long been used to indicate the strength or weakness of a union: The smaller the loss of jobs with a 5 percent wage increase, the stronger the union, runs the argument.

---

4   The change must be "small" for two reasons: (1) If the applicable curve is not linear but bending, the percentage method will introduce an error because it rests on the assumption of straight lines; and (2) the percentages obtained for the same line segment of a curve will diverge according to whether the wage rate is increased or decreased.

5   Thus the absolute elasticity of labor demand $= RQ/QP$ in the first case, and SQ/QP in the second.

The Marshall Argument for the Greater Strength of Craft Unions

Nearly a century ago, Alfred Marshall, the great British economist, employed the following argument to resolve the question of the determinants of comparative union power [12, pp. 381-393]. His procedure was both sophisticated and complex, because it linked together the labor market for the services of the members of a particular union, say, the Plumbers; the market for the final product obtained partly from those services—a house or a building; and finally the market for the other factors of production cooperating in the process—capital and other types of labor. The analysis can be applied to both the single firm and to the industry of which it is a part. The upshot of Marshall's argument is that where certain unusual conditions prevail, the absolute elasticity values along the demand curve for plumber craftsmen, for example, will be less for a unit increase of wage rate than for a weaker union. In short, it will be steeply tilted.

True, the demand curve for labor will have the usual negative slope; but what matters is whether the slope is steep or very slight. All "ordinary" demand curves have negative slopes. What is peculiar about the demand curves for the services of craftsmen in strong unions is that their demand slopes are typically steep, while those for unskilled workers are very gradual. Indeed, the principle has since been applied to industrial unions [6, pp. 155-161. For criticism, see 16, pp. 384-401]. In short, the demand curve for plumbers' services will be much steeper than for the weaker groups. Thus, as Fig. 5.7 shows, the stronger union can impose the same given wage increase in cents per hour as a weaker group, but with a much smaller derivative unemployment. To Marshall, these were the basic signs of union strength.

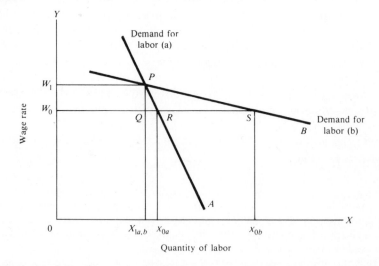

Fig. 5.7 Comparative absolute elasticities of demand for labor for the same change in the wage rate.

In his view of the matter, four factors jointly must be present to provide a union with demand conditions represented by a curve of the highly favorable A type in Fig. 5.7. Moreover, it was also his opinion that highly skilled craft groups were most likely to enjoy these conditions, and thus be able to force up wages with impunity. (1) The labor services supplied through the union must be "essential" in the sense that there is very little possibility for technical substitution, E_s, that is, for replacement by a cheaper input beyond the union's effective control. Here the basic idea is that no machine or process can be introduced, even over the long run, to permit the employer to dispense with the skills of the group. In this respect, the plumbers' trade is an excellent example. There is simply no way to replace the skills required to cut, thread, and join pipe to bring into being a functional and leak-proof system without recourse to the composite skills of the pipe fitter. Furthermore, each job is "tailor made" even though certain parts are standardized. Because the pipefitting skill is irreplaceable, the wage level for such work makes no real difference, viewed separately from Marshall's other factors. For the same reason, this powerful technical advantage is one reason why the United Association in the American pipe trades is within the top rank on the pay scale.[6]

(2) Marshall's second factor is that the final product in which the services of the craftsmen are incorporated must also have a low long-run elasticity of demand, E_d. This means that an increase in price for the product will bring relatively little reduction in quantity sold; thus a craft union may force up its wage rate. This in turn forces up costs, and through costs, as we have shown, the supply price of the product. But because the elasticity of demand for the product is low, there is little loss of sales. For the same reason, there is little loss of employment for the craft group: The demand curve has so steep a slope. In essence, Marshall's second factor says that with highly inelastic product demand the response of relative quantity (employment) to a relative wage change is comparatively much smaller.[7] As we shall see later, this principle has much to do with the emergence of "association" or industrywide bargaining, which takes several forms in the United States, but in all cases rests upon the fact that the elasticity of demand for a product is less for an entire industry than for a single firm in that industry.

(3) Marshall's third factor contributing to a steeply sloping demand for labor operates when the union in question accounts for a very low proportion of total costs of production, C, of the product of the firm or industry. The

---

6   The full title is the United Association of Journeymen and Apprentices of the Plumbing and Pipe Fitting Industry of the United States and Canada. Only the Air Line Pilots Association is likely to exceed the Plumbers in annual earnings. Significantly, the Plumbers have only about 225,000 members.

7   It is tempting to say that labor demand here should be zero-elastic, because all buildings require plumbing. But buyers can adjust the quantity of plumbing they choose to install; hence wages are a factor.

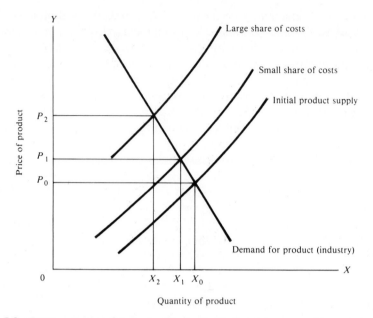

Fig. 5.8 Displacement of industry product supply curve according to share of wages in total costs.

basic principle is intuitively simple: Although a given wage increase will normally be passed through to force up the product supply curve, the degree of this upward displacement will be directly associated with the proportion of wages to total costs, as is indicated in Fig. 5.8. With a low wage share, the loss in sales is only $X_0 - X_1$; but when the share is substantial, the loss in sales (and jobs for union members) is $X_0 - X_2$. Even with the same wage increase, more jobs would be lost.

Note, further, that given the share of wages in total costs, the *slope* of the product demand curve for the industry determines the number of jobs lost. However, whatever the slope of the product curve, a low wage share will bring about a smaller drop in sales and employment than will a higher share. In consequence, the demand curve for craft labor has a steeper slope at all points if its share of total costs is small. For the same reasons, the demand for semiskilled industrial labor will be more elastic at all points, because its share is usually much greater. This principle serves as an important prop for the contention by some economists today that industrial unions are inherently weaker than most of those of the craft type.[8]

---

8   However, as Ulman [16] has pointed out, in many industries craft unions work together—construction, printing, newspapers, railroads, and entertainment, for example. In these cases it is their *aggregate* share of total costs that matters. Since it may well range between 40 and 60 percent, the advantage of smallness is lost.

(4) Marshall's final factor is the most subtle of them all. It says that if the supply curves, E_c, of the other factors that cooperate in production with this particular craft are highly inelastic (with respect to their prices), then the given craft, by pushing up its own wages, can "squeeze" or force down the demand curves for these other inputs, lowering their returns accordingly. In result, the strong craft can extract more wages without necessarily forcing up the product supply curve of the industry at all, and therefore without significant loss of jobs for its own members. In short, low elasticities of supply for cooperating inputs contribute to low elasticities of demand for the services of the craft group in question.

Probably the best example of the fourth factor at work is in industries using large quantities of fixed capital, such as railroads or basic steel mills. Since this capital is "sunk" and has no mobility until returns fall so low as to make scrapping an alternative, the employers may choose to respond to a wage increase not by raising supply prices for the product, particularly where competition makes product demand quite elastic, but by reducing returns to capital because its supply curve is almost vertical, as in Fig. 5.9. This takes the form of reduced or suspended dividends, failure to pay interest, and over the long run, a gradual consumption of capital. Where such a squeeze can be applied—to capital or to unorganized workers in an isolated location—the demand elasticities for the powerful union will be considerably lower because the effect of the squeezing is to create "wage space" for the strong union, essentially through a failure of the product

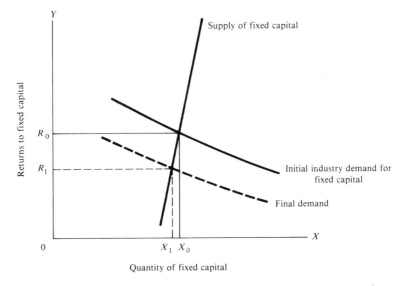

Fig. 5.9 Squeezing the fixed factor in an industry to absorb a wage increase imposed by a strong union.

supply curve of the industry to rise when a wage increase is won. Their costs go down while those for the craft group go up.[9]

Time, however, can be the weakening agent that ultimately is likely to debilitate the strongest organizations—not by its mere passing, but in the sense that the greater the amount of time available for adjustment by entrepreneurs and consumers to the wage pressure exerted by a strongly situated union, the greater will be the ultimate relative job loss. Put another way, the demand curve for the services of the union's members will become less steep over its whole range when more time is available.[10] Substitute products may tilt the product demand curve for the industry. Mechanization and other innovations may significantly increase technical substitution for the work of craftsmen. New nonunion firms may enter the industry; old firms may quit or move to locations beyond the union's reach.

This analysis can be applied to other cases as well. Consider, for example, the position of an industrial union, say, in the automobile or steel industries. Because its ranks will include many workers with little or no skill, the union will be highly vulnerable to technical substitution in the form of mechanization and new machines. Beyond this adverse factor, the wage bill of the union will likely be a substantial percentage of total costs in the industry, and further, because the union includes all wage occupations, there will be no other groups of workers for the union to squeeze for its own gains.[11] Thus, even if product demand slopes were the same in the two cases, the craft union would run less risk of creating substantial unemployment than would the industrial one under the conditions stated.

Some economists go so far as to say that only craft unions can be considered "strong" in the sense of having a wage advantage. Three reasons are given for this: the crafts will have a lower long-run absolute elasticity of derived demand for their services; they are able to control the supply of required labor through their ability to wage effective strikes and through their control of access of new employees to the trade by devices such as apprenticeship regulations; and through their ability to enforce their wage scale upon existing employers as well as new entrants. Out of the entire labor force, the argument runs, probably not over 10 percent are in unions with these peculiar advantages.

---

9   The firms in an industry in this predicament may consider it inexpedient to raise prices at all, in which case we have $\bar{C} = \uparrow W_c L_c + \downarrow W_u L_u + KR$. This says that total costs (C) are fixed; that craft wages (W_c) are raised; that unskilled wages (W_u) are lowered; and that the rate of return (R) on sunk capital (K) will be depressed enough to satisfy the total cost limitation, yet allow a craft wage increase. Obviously this case has more weight in the short run.

10   Indeed, the demand curve may also shift leftward as well as becoming more elastic.

11   Some squeezing of fixed capital could be done, but not over the long run, for it would leave the industry or be scrapped.

It should be evident that the central concern of this analysis is with the factors that affect the ability of certain unions to bend the wage structure in their favor—an analysis that is concentrated upon the long-run elasticity of derived demand for particular kinds of labor. The few craft unions that enjoy this wage advantage by no means exhaust the list of all crafts. At the same time, however, another conclusion is also suggested: The many industrial unions with their millions of members are basically "weak." They enjoy few wage advantages because market conditions supposedly do not favor them.

But is this actually the case? If we rest the answer upon what is probably the most thorough study ever made of the comparative effects of unionism upon wages [11], the answer seems to be that "it depends." If we consider the average overall wage of union labor relative to that of nonunion labor, then, depending upon the period in time, the percentage wage advantage for union labor ranged from over 25 percent during 1931-33 to 15-20 percent in 1923-29, and to only 0-5 percent during 1945-49.[12] For the most recent period studied, 1957-58, the estimated impact is 10-15 percent [11, p. 193].

However, these are overall comparisons, while what we have just been discussing is the comparative strength of unions *relative to each other*. The two issues of course are not unrelated, but here they should be distinguished. After a review of numerous other studies, Lewis finds the evidence "quite inconclusive" regarding any demonstrated advantages for craft unionism, particularly involving the skilled, or for high concentration of industry output as among a relatively few producers [11, pp. 284, 285].

The Comparative Strength of Unions in Recent Times

Accepting the inconclusive state of our present knowledge, it is still worthwhile to attempt some impressionistic judgments. What the elasticity analysis says essentially is that a strong union is such because it confronts the "right" kind of labor demand curve. In addition, either this curve must be stable or it must move gradually outward and upward without much loss of slope, because the industry is a growing one. Unions that enjoy these characteristics should display a wage advantage of over 15 percent.

Two additional considerations enter at this point. One is obvious: The union must have the ability to strike and to strike effectively by holding its ranks together. Thus the strike can serve as a credible threat to be held in reserve during negotiations. When brought into play it must close down the employer's operations so that the costs involved will push him toward settlement.

The other consideration concerns the scope of the union's negotiating "reach" over the product market, which is just as essential as the ability to

---

12   Union money wages are well known to be rigid downward, owing to the traditional "no-cuts" policy of organized labor. Hence the large relative spread in 1931-33.

strike itself. In short, the union must have its trade or industry fully organized. Indeed, it is but another way of talking about the elasticity of demand for the final product, E_L. Finally, it is what unionists themselves have always had in mind when they speak of the necessity for "taking wages out of competition."

A simple example will demonstrate the point. Assume that a union has been recognized for bargaining purposes by a monopolist. By definition it enjoys full coverage of the relevant product market. It need fear no nonunion employers when it enters into negotiations, because there exist no other sellers who could undercut the monopolist's price. In other words, for this union there is no problem of incomplete organization of the labor market because the relevant labor market is identical with the labor force employed by the monopolist and represented by the union in its negotiations with him. For the same reason, the strike-effectiveness of the union is at its maximum, for it has no competing firms to worry about.

As this example indicates, what every union attempts to achieve is recognition by all of the firms that compete in a given product market, followed by permanent bargaining relations, so that it can then strive for standard wages, fringe benefits, and basic working conditions in all of its contracts. We may term this objective *full occupancy of the relevant product market*. The necessary counterpart of this condition—indeed, the means by which it is achieved—*is complete organization of the relevant labor market*. When there exists this perfect match-up between its degree of organization in the two markets, and when in addition all of the contracts with the employers expire at about the same time, the union can be said to have attained its maximum bargaining effectiveness for the time being.

The notions of full occupancy and complete organization provide us with a very useful ideal type or conceptual norm with which to identify the principal sources of strength and weakness in the bargaining effectiveness of unions over short periods.[13] They also throw much light upon organizing strategies.

Why has full occupancy of the product market been considered so vital for so many years by trade union leaders?

One way to find the answer is to consider the main source of bargaining weakness in a union, namely, incomplete organization of the relevant labor market, and indirectly through this the relevant product market. This situation can take various forms. For example, in the textile trade it has never been possible to organize all of the domestic employers and plants, particularly with the southward migration of the industry that began some

---

13 We say "short periods" because it takes considerable time for technical substitution against labor to become significant, and because the squeezing of fixed factors is also a slow process. Thus it is product-demand elasticity that matters in the short run.

sixty years ago. By comparison, the apparel industry has undergone a similar experience but has also suffered from the additional handicap of unusually easy entry of new nonunion firms. Then, finally, incomplete organization can also emerge as the passive consequence of an increase of imports of competitive goods—"passive" in the sense that even if domestic organization is virtually 100 percent at the outset, a surge of competing imports can open up an uncontrolled margin of product supply, since the unions have no direct control over foreign wages and import prices.

Whatever the reason for incomplete organization, its typical effect is to make it much more difficult for a union to negotiate wage increases because relative employment losses will be made much greater. In other words, the elasticity of demand for labor for any firm in the unionized component of the industry is substantially larger than it would be if the union has achieved full occupancy. Figure 5.10 illustrates the general situation. Demand elasticities for the product are much higher at any price if the union does not have all firms and their plants under bargaining control. The source for such weakness, of course, is the existence of a nonunion component whose labor costs are likely to be lower and more flexible. In consequence the demand curve for labor in a unionized firm will also be more elastic, lying somewhat closer to the origin and having a more gradual average slope. Given these circumstances, the union can have the higher wage, W_1, but only at the cost of leaving a substantial number of workers unemployed. Alternatively, it can choose a lower wage, W_0, increasing its force from A to S, but only by sacrificing some of its wage advantage, bringing the negotiated wage down closer to the unorganized one. On the same ground, the union will be seriously hampered in trying to achieve wage W_1, because this would cripple the "good" (unionized) employers by imposing higher costs upon them, relative to their nonunion competitors.

Figure 5.10 is also a useful way to visualize the contemporary problem of imports, with its adverse effects for both unions and their members and for employers. Before the recent substantial upsurge in imports of basic steel, for example, the United Steelworkers had the industry fully organized, and imports were of no great consequence. With the flood of additional imports, each firm in the domestic branch of the industry began confronting a downward shifting and much more elastic product demand curve. The Steelworkers underwent a similar experience. With negotiated wages holding at W_1, employment fell from S to Q.[14] Reduced production schedules, mill closures, layoffs, calls for antidumping restrictions, and demands for quotas all followed.

---

14 As an artifice, we treat the A curve in the lower panel of Fig. 5.10 as the new, downshifted labor demand curve invoked by the imports.

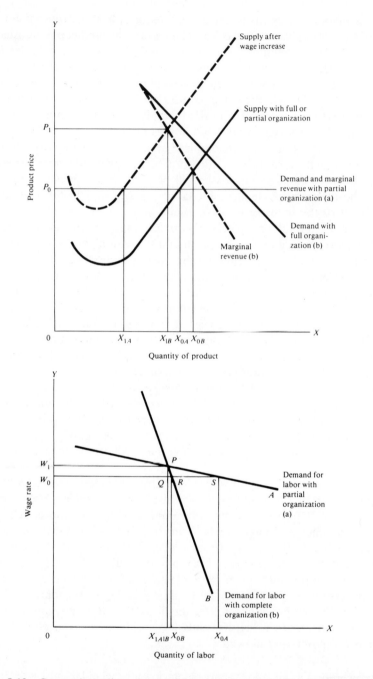

Fig. 5.10   Comparison of product and labor markets for a firm in an industry that is fully or partially organized. In the upper panel, the two firms are assumed to have identical supply (marginal cost) curves: The solid line represents supply before the wage increase; the broken line, supply after the wage increase.

So far we have considered two main sources of bargaining weakness: situations in which the union has never succeeded in gaining full occupancy or even dominance in the industry and situations in which full occupancy has been won in the domestic industry only to be undermined during the past decade or more by imports. In effect, the real industry in these cases is international in scope, while the limits of the bargaining reach of the domestic union are to be found at the national boundaries.

However, there is still another source of weakness, whose effects are formally similar to the others, but whose origins are different. In this instance, the problem involves the entry of new nonunion firms that undercut the position of the union and its organized employers. For this process to operate, conditions of entry must be relatively easy. To illustrate, capital requirements must be low, technology must be readily accessible, raw materials must be available, and the unions must be unable to impose barriers.

A surprising instance of invasion of a tightly organized industry by new firms is to be found in construction—surprising because the construction trades have been a citadel of American unionism for almost a century. The incursion of new firms is now at least a decade old. It includes both large general contractors, often operating on an international scale, and a variety of specialty contractors as well (plumbing, heating, electrical, etc.). There would seem to be two basic reasons for this development, one legal and one economic.

On the legal side, Secton 8(b)(4)(A) of the Taft-Hartley Act of 1947 outlawed the secondary boycott, that is, the technique of bringing pressure to bear on third parties to get at the union's real target in the dispute—for example, by refusing to handle certain goods or by picketing to shut down an innocent employer in order to injure his or her suppliers or purchasers. In the *Denver Building and Construction Trades* case, in which a group of pickets from several crafts shut down an entire job by picketing the general contractor for doing business with a nonunion electrical specialty contractor, the Supreme Court rejected the unions' claim that the specialty contractors were not independent "innocents" but really were agents of a single employer, the general contractor. By this finding, the Court brought the secondary boycott rule to bear [14] against the construction trades, in a finding that ultimately was to weaken drastically the ability of these unions to engage in coercive organizing of employees and to shut out nonunion firms through complete control of the job site.

On the economic side, the building trades unintentionally may have created a strong incentive over the past decade for nonunion contractors to get into the business. Given the local nature of construction bargaining, together with the boom in building and the tight system of union control over labor supply (closed shop, regulation of numbers of helpers and apprentices), increases in wage rates and fringe benefits began to show a runaway pattern. By the early 1970s hourly increases of 15 to 18 percent annually were common, although this process has since subsided. Although some of the national leaders viewed these developments with increasing concern, they were virtually powerless to control local settlements.

As labor costs soared, the nonunion contractors gained an important indirect advantage: Because they were free of craft work-separation rules, they could make substantial savings on excess labor requirements and idle time. In particular, the large general contractors found themselves able to underbid on industrial and commercial jobs, offer their crews permanent jobs, and yet pay wages comparable to those enjoyed by union workers. At the same time, small builders in residential construction found it possible to take over more than half the industry, even obtaining union craftsmen who were prepared to overlook their affiliations simply to get steady work. It would seem, therefore, that market forces ultimately do check increasing union relative wage spreads.

From what we have said so far, it follows that imports and easy entry—both of which make for much higher elasticities of labor demand through their similar effect upon product demand—are the principal weakening agents for the bargaining power of unions. But this view leaves matters incomplete, because within many parts of manufacturing and extractive industry entry of new firms rarely takes place, while union occupancy is virtually complete. Here the number of competing firms is small; thus the product market is oligopolistic and concentration of market shares is typically high. On average since World War II, profit rates have been good (around 12 percent on investment) and unionism has been firmly established ever since World War II.

In this sort of case, one encounters a paradox. On the one side, the financial resources of the large corporations involved, indeed, their very size itself, suggest that they have exceptional power to resist the demands of a strong union. On the other, the union need not fear invasion of the product market by new nonunion firms, because technology and market scope impose such large capital requirements.[15] Thus it would seem that the main threat from substitution confronting a union in these circumstances is technical—the long-run replacement of labor by capital in the input structure of the industry. This, of course, would increase labor-demand elasticity, but only over lengthy periods, during which any consequential unemployment could well be concealed by "normal" economic growth of sales and production. At the same time, by increasing labor productivity per man-hour, the rising capital-to-labor ratios would continuously restore a margin of "wage space" to absorb a steadily rising trend of negotiated wage rates, benefits, and working conditions. Union-management cooperation to reduce costs can also contribute in this direction.

---

15   For a review and evaluation of studies of the problem, see Levinson [10, pp. 198-201].

In any case, it is by no means obvious that unions in these industries are necessarily weak in bargaining relative to their employers, provided that they have achieved full occupancy and complete organization and that imports do not offer an immediate threat of substantial commodity substitution with an attendant increase in labor-demand elasticity.

Consider now a quite puzzling case, that of the railroads. Again, the factors that supposedly dictate union weakness are all present: relatively few firms, lack of new entrants, and a shrinking overall market share. Even more, unionism in this industry is of the multiple craft type: there are 18 labor organizations that represent the half-million employees involved. Yet, notwithstanding these apparent management advantages, when we examine the record of the past three decades, we find that average railroad wages have been rising at a trend rate that puts the industry almost at the top of the list, with labor productivity also displaying exceptional trend rates of gain until very recently.

In contrast with these developments, the industry has lost almost all of its passenger business while its freight volume has been rising very slowly, with a sharp decline in its relative share of the intercity market. On the labor side, nearly 800,000 jobs have been wiped out—about 60 percent of the 1947 total. Clearly, the railroad unions have been willing to trade off job opportunities on a massive scale in exchange for substantially higher wages for the surviving incumbents. At the same time, they have been unusually successful in exploiting the inelasticity of supply of the fixed capital with which they work—compelling the companies to accept ever lower rates of return as a way of absorbing the costs of higher wages.

Despite the size and financial resources of the typical employer in big industry, the unions in these fields on the whole have been able to cope very effectively. There has been no substantial empirical showing so far to suggest that unionism has been weaker in these industries than in the craft group, as Lewis concluded from his own study [11]. The secret of their success can be interpreted, if not demonstrated with quantitative precision, by recourse to the earlier discussion of elasticity.

Consider, first, elasticity of demand for the product. It will necessarily be lower for an entire industry than for a single firm. In consequence, the unions have pressed for what in substance, if not always in form, are industrywide bargaining and settlements—by sequential imposition of a pattern (automobiles, copper), by dealing with a joint committee of employers (basic steel), or by a formal employer association (railroads). In all cases the unions have been able to impose a large measure of contractual uniformity upon each of these very important industries.

As for Marshall's second factor—"essentiality" of the labor input (degree of technical substitution)—it can be said *a priori* that its elasticity is higher in these industries than in certain craft trades such as the plumbers and electricians. But except for railroads, technical substitution has not been so great as to produce large-scale displacement of workers. Rather, it has contributed to rising productivity and higher real wages, and therefore has been helpful to the unions. However, on the railroads it has been partially responsible for the massive loss of jobs since World War II, although it has also done much to make substantial wage gains possible.

Regarding Marshall's third factor—ratio of labor to total costs—the variance in this measure is great over the entire range of industry, but in those we have mentioned the proportion is quite substantial. This, of course, is a negative factor for any union, but when the *combined* cost shares of a group of cooperating craft unions are considered, as in printing and newspaper publishing, construction, and longshoring and maritime shipping, the presumed advantage of the craft union becomes more apparent than real.

Finally, there is the fourth factor—the elasticity of supply of cooperating inputs in production. Here, typically, the principal cooperant is capital (including land). And because large-scale industry commonly involves "sunk" or fixed capital, it follows that, for the short run at least, its elasticity is near zero. In short, unions in this branch of the economy can "exploit" the fixed factor, as was just noted for railroads, driving down its returns to extract higher wages—clearly an advantage for the labor side. In turn, management is induced to accelerate the technical substitution of capital for labor to protect capital returns as best it can.

With a few exceptions, it does not seem that craft unions generally have an inherent advantage over their industrial union counterparts, or that typical craft industries—building, printing, and so on—generally show wage levels and profiles superior to those of large-scale industry. Thus at this point Lewis's judgment that the evidence is inconclusive appears in order.

However, the story does not really end here. For what has been happening to important sections of big industry over the past 15 years has been a steady growth of imports, now at levels of 20 percent or more in industries such as steel, automobiles, and copper. In short, the movement, as well as the elasticity, of product demand both have become increasingly adverse. Through foreign trade, in other words, the large industrial unions have witnessed the opening up of a major gap in their effective occupancy and organization of their markets. The same effects have been felt on the railroads, although from a different source—the displacement of demands for their services by the competitive inroads of air and truck transportation, which represent the gap problem in another form. But to complete the picture, adverse shifts in product demand have also been felt in some of the craft industries. In construction, for example, the large-scale entry of new firms—from major general contractors to small general and specialty builders—has posed the problem of incomplete labor market organization with a vengeance.

So to sum up, competition remains a powerful force throughout most of the American economy. Or, in the language of Sir John Hicks, "Capitalist enterprise is the child of evasion; and on the long road from ancient smuggler to modern industrialist, the entrepreneur has learned more tricks than are easily reckoned with" [9, p. 229].

To round out our assessment of the comparative power of unions in the labor markets in which they operate, we ought now to consider a third distinct category of industries. As with those in our first group—textiles, apparel, and shoes—these industries also are characterized by apparent ease of entry, large numbers of competing firms, and in some cases by flexibility in product prices. A hasty inference would be that this group belongs in the first category, and this would be true except for one very important difference: Both in level and in trend rate of increase, wages in these industries have performed just as well as in the well-publicized steel and automobile industries—in other words, far better than in the first category of atomistic industries. The problem is, Why?[16]

Once again the answer is to be sought in degrees of occupancy and organization of the relevant product and labor markets, and above all, obstacles to the entry of new competition.

The industries in question include motor freight, longshoring and seafaring, construction, newspaper publishing, and activities such as theatrical and musical entertainment. In each instance, the secret of union power, as Levinson has suggested, lies in what he terms "the spatial limitations of the physical area within which new entrants can effectively produce" [10, p. 202]. These limitations provide a special kind of barrier whose effect is to limit entry, participation, and numbers in the industry just as high capital requirements or technology make for concentration in large-scale manufacturing or mining or public utilities. In consequence, the entry of new nonunion competitors is usually not a problem for the unions involved. For the same reason, degree of occupancy and organization is not a problem.

Consider the nature of these spatial limitations. In motor freight, the Teamsters union controls the loading dock, and through this the interchange, assembly, and break-up of cargo. Any putative nonunion carrier would have to duplicate all of these facilities and to collect all of its own business without cooperation from other carriers and cartage concerns—obviously an enormous and highly risky undertaking.

In longshoring and seafaring, the problem is substantially the same for the potential new entrant. The longshore unions control the "skin of the dock" and adjacent sheds and these are the points of ingress and egress for ocean freight. Any new business venture must first establish its legitimacy within this vital piece of territory. In construction, the problem is access to the job site by nonunion general or specialty contractors. To enter effectively, the general contractor either has to bring in his own group of specialists, as an integrated firm, so to speak, or attempt to recruit nonunion

---

16   This problem was first raised by Levinson [10].

specialty contractors—all this in a confined site where arson and violence are not unknown as weapons to enforce "control of turf."

In musical and theatrical productions, the would-be nonunion producer confronts problems essentially the same as in construction. There exists an entrenched set of crafts, each with a well-defined piece of "turf" at each of the halls and theaters. There is no practical way to set up a competitive entertainment venture.

The illustrations are sufficient to make the central point: Entry can be controlled by spatial demarcation in industries that otherwise would be comparable to textiles. Such control can be achieved by industrial as well as craft unions; thus the form of the union is not the critical factor, although unions of the craft type seem to predominate in this third category of industries. What *is* important is limitation of numbers, the need of every producer to gain access to the product market, and the ability of the union to control such access.

THE MACROECONOMIC SIDE OF UNIONISM AND WAGES

Some Direct Impacts of Unionism on the Economy as a Whole

In their functioning as economic agencies, labor unions operate on the microeconomic level. Moreover, they represent only 25 percent of all employees, and not more than a third of all employees in the private sector. Nonetheless, unionism has acquired major importance for the behavior and management of the entire economy.

Before examining the overall impacts of unionism, it should be pointed out that the general view today is that unions typically establish their wage premium over nonunion groups very early in their histories. It is in this sense that they produce a cost-push form of inflation. Thereafter they reestablish this premium with each successive contract, in delayed reaction to inflation rather than as initiating cause. The long-run overall rate of inflation is an independent process for which union wage setting is much more effect than cause.

Where unionism and collective bargaining prevail, wages, hours, and other conditions of work become embodied in contracts. These contracts usually run for one to three years. On the one side, they impart a degree of stability—critics would say "stickiness" or inflexibility—to the labor market. On the other, they make for discrete changes each time a new settlement is reached. Or, put a little differently, changes in wages occur sharply and then are followed by a lengthy period of stability until the next negotiation comes around. Compared with the stock market or grain exchange, where prices are fully flexible and change from instant to instant, wage setting with unions is a discontinuous process involving administered prices that are inflexible downward. However, they may be adjusted upward from time to time during the life of the agreement, under COLA (cost-of-living clauses) or through built-in annual increases.

It should also be noted—indeed, it was pointed out as far back as 1897 by Sidney and Beatrice Webb [19, pp. 279-323] that when unions negotiate over wages, their goal is a standard job rate for each type of work, a rate that is to be distinguished from personal rates paid to individuals. For the typical craft union, there is but one primary job rate, that paid the journeyman with the requisite skill qualifications. Apprentice and helper rates are then linked to this key rate. By contrast, in plant unionism there will normally be found a whole complex of job rates, grouped into lines of progression or "job ladders." At the bottom of each ladder is a starting job that has an entry-level rate. These entry-rate jobs are tied closely to the labor market external to the plant because this market is the main source of supply of new workers. By contrast, the rates for the higher-level jobs in the complex are associated with the internal labor market of the plant. For these reasons they are much less sensitive to changes in external conditions of the labor market. It has also been suggested that these internal rates are never technically in equlibrium. They are not market-clearing rates because the number of qualified candidates normally exceeds the number of vacancies. In result job opportunities have to be rationed by other means, usually seniority.

The discontinuity imposed by long-term agreements carries several implications, although our knowledge of these is still incomplete. One of the most important is the lag problem for stabilization policy intended to control inflation and unemployment [3, p. 387; 18, p. 517]. In short, a contract is determined by influences coming to bear at a finite point in time. However, the wage provisions so determined are built in for the life of an agreement, and may well exert their influence long after, say, three or more years later, when markedly changed conditions prevail in the economic environment—new circumstances that call for different responses from those already incorporated in the agreement. To illustrate, a three-year contract drafted during boom conditions may provide for large annual increases in each of the two succeeding years, although a serious recession may have set in in the meantime. In result, built-in increases in labor costs can become extremely burdensome to management, bringing about substantial layoffs as well.

Labor contracts, of course, are not executed in isolation: They come in bunches or clusters, and they are often interdependent, sometimes highly so, for reasons that include not only market forces but what might be called the politics of wage setting under collective bargaining. Among the market factors would be connections betweeen supplier and user industries that cause them to prosper or to suffer together, geographic sharing of labor markets, and the existence of a pattern for wage changes, such as cans and basic steel [3, p. 385]. The pattern will in turn reflect rivalries among unions and their leaders, such that it becomes an "orbit of coercive comparison" (Arthur M. Ross) for all of the organizations involved. This is not to say that all labor contracts in the United States (which probably exceed 175,000) follow a single pattern, although in times of protracted inflation such as today, the "going annual increase" is universal throughout the collective bargaining system.[17] In any case, the orbit theory emphasizes administrative and political processes, and notions of equity. By contrast, some economists have argued that these "coercive orbits" are illusory. They actually reflect parallel conditions of excess labor demand extending across several industries. In this view, then, the patterns of increase reflect market forces.

Bringing matters together, we can say that through contracts, fixed job rates, COLA adjustments, annual increases, and expanding fringe benefits, unionism introduces a one-way upward plasticity along with downward rigidity to that part of the wage system embraced by labor agreements.

However, the union sector is by no means the whole of the American economy, for it is accompanied by a competitive sector in which there is no collective bargaining. During periods of sustained inflation, there is some spillover of increases from the high-wage union sector, although the transfer is less than one-for-one. Even here there is some stickiness to wage rates on the downside, but during marked recessions the rate of spillover slows down, which in turn widens the gap of wage advantage in favor of the unionized group. During booms, the opposite holds true: Expanding demand pulls up wages more readily in the nonunion sector while contract lags slow the rate of advance for the union group.

Unionism as a Political Force for Inflation

Although unions such as the Auto Workers, Steelworkers, Machinists, Teamsters, and Plumbers have had the market power to extract substantial increases in wages and benefits year after year, it would be a serious mistake to attribute inflation solely to collective bargaining, or to unions and big corporations together. The error in such reasoning is that it confuses the parts with the whole, or *particular* wages and prices with the *levels* of all wages and prices—call it the price level for short. At any one time, the whole price level is determined by the ratio between the quantity of money times the speed of its turnover, divided by the volume of trade (output) [4, pp. 149-183. This ratio is convenient shorthand for classifying the principal channels of causation affecting the price level.]. In short, the price level reflects the fundamental relationship between the quantity of money and the volume of goods in the whole economy.

---

17   Eckstein and Wilson found that wage settlements occurred in "rounds" from start to completion, and that a central group, which included rubber, primary and fabricated metals, electrical and nonelectrical machinery, and transportation equipment, showed matching increases in round after round. Econometrically, the unemployment and profit rates explained these movements almost completely. In the 15 years following their study, the government sector has emerged with patterns of its own, such as among teachers, policemen, and firemen.

In other words, the price level and its inflation are monetary phenomena. To illustrate the principle, if the entire unionized sector were to negotiate a 10 percent increase in its wage level, offset by no increase in labor productivity, then the only ways in which this could force up the price level would be through an enforced decrease in output or a parallel increase in the money supply.[18] If output falls in the unionized sector, the workers who are made unemployed either would migrate to the nonunion sector to find jobs, which would press down wages and prices in that sector, or would queue up awaiting recall, similar to the processes shown in Figs. 5.4 and 5.5. Further, if higher prices emerged in the union sector and these caused a diversion of expenditure to union goods, there would be a drop in outlay in the nonunion sector, with a further fall in prices there. In the upshot, therefore, the rise in the price level as a whole would be choked off *unless* the monetary authorities choose to increase the quantity of money in circulation. But the only reason for them to do this would be to reduce unemployment and increase output in the union sector. To do this would be to underwrite or *validate* the unions' original negotiated wage increase, that is, to cancel out any unemployment arising from it. The heart of the matter is that this requires an increase in the supply of money, which is the reason for describing inflation as a monetary rather than a wage-push phenomenon.

Figure 5.11 summarizes the argument. If full employment exists with a given level of total demand, D_1, a given level of wage costs, OS_1, in the right-hand panel will indicate average cost per unit of output, FG/OF. If the wage level could be pushed up by the unions, OS_2 becomes the new aggregate supply curve, but full employment at OF is sacrificed and UF unemployment is created. By larger deficit spending and/or direct increase in money, aggregate demand, initially D_1 in the right-hand panel, is increased by government action to D_2: UF is canceled out, full employment is restored or maintained, but average price per unit of product, now FH/OF, has risen. Thus monetary expansion "accommodates" wage policy. Overall inflation is the result.

This brings us to the core of the postwar wage problem: the systematic inflation of the wage and fringe benefit level in the union sector, aided by other political advantages sought by organized labor, among them higher minimum wages, higher minimum craft rates on federal construction, and higher unemployment compensation and social security. To keep the gap of rising money wage costs relative to increased ouput per man-hour from creating substantial unemployment, federal fiscal and monetary policy has been highly expansionary. This has been achieved through the commitment of the government to full employment. Although that commitment, first expressed in the Employment Act of 1946, has always enjoyed a broad

---

18 We may ignore changes in velocity for purposes of the argument.

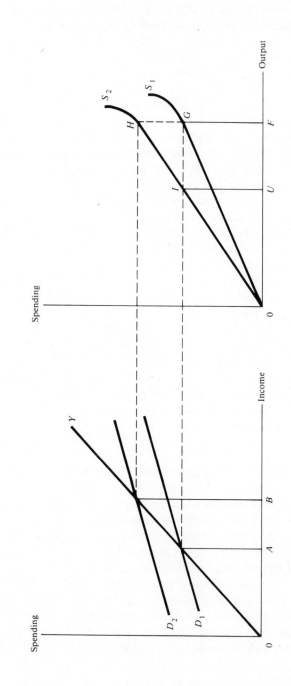

Fig. 5.11   Wage-push inflation as validated by monetary expansion to sustain full employment. (Adapted from Gordon |8, pp. 70-71|.)

measure of popular support, it is safe to say that the labor movement has always been its strongest and most articulate advocate.

The Employment Act of 1946 spoke only of the goal of "high employment" without accompanying inflation. It did not stipulate a specific target figure for the maximum general rate of unemployment associated uniquely with full employment. At that time, 3 percent was the target rate here and in England, but by the early 1960s the Kennedy administration began speaking of a minimum attainable "interim" rate of 4 percent. Within three years, inflation began to accelerate under the spending required for the war in Vietnam and for the Great Society programs. With these developments, the notion of a minimum noninflationary rate of general unemployment began to lose precision as well as broad acceptance by professional economists, until today the range is indicated at somewhere between 4.5 and 6 percent, but without much conviction.

Nonetheless, the sense of moral commitment to some level of "full" employment has continued high on the agenda for federal policy. Along with it there also survives a still strong although now dwindling professional faith in the old Keynesian doctrine that increased deficit spending by the federal government is the principal if not the exclusive method for bringing down our stubbornly high unemployment rates of recent years at least to 6 percent if not less [2].

The link from the labor movement through deficit spending to inflation has been readily apparent for some thirty years, although it can hardly be denied that the middle term—increased deficit spending for new programs and bigger existing ones—is by no means the exclusive handiwork of organized labor. Plenty of businessmen have the same outlook, as well as farmers and professional groups. In essence, it is still the central economic doctrine of the voting majority, and it reflects a whole panoply of special interests, each of which will gain more by pressing for its particular program than it could hope to get from the exercise of self-restraint.

But what does unionism get from big programs financed by deficit spending? In the narrow sense, of course, the construction trades obtain much employment from public-works projects. But from a really broad point of view, deficit spending, especially when financed by the Federal Reserve banks, fosters a more rapid increase in the money supply, because it adds to the primary reserves and thus the lending capacity of the commercial banks. As Fisher's equation so well describes it, money expands to prevent the fall in "trade" (output) that a rise in wages and prices pushed by the "unions and the trusts" otherwise would bring about. Or, in more modern language, excessively rapid expansion of money—say, in the name of full employment—makes possible an inflationary wage policy for the unions, buoyant markets for farmers, merchants, and industrialists, and all this without sizable concomitant unemployment or disemployment because both product and labor markets are made more buoyant. However, it is far less certain that these policies have had detectable beneficial effects for real wages.

For three decades we have been following an easy money policy, one of whose consequences has been a rise in money wages well in excess of the trend rate of improvement in gross labor output per man-hour. Another consequence has been an inflation of the whole price level. Yet, save for a very few brief periods, the general unemployment rate has been stuck at about 5 percent. Over the past five years, the range has been between 6 and over 9 percent, always accompanied by inflation.

The foregoing analysis suggests strongly that the unions do not "cause" general inflation by forcing up particular wages. Rather, they provide an important part of the powerful political support for fiscal and monetary policies that bring about excessively rapid increases in money wages for all employees, along with persistent and often severe general price inflation. Given a 30-year commitment to full employment, government policy has rendered the unions almost completely immune to the classical penalty for uneconomic wage increases—namely, higher unemployment. Thus the recurring gains in money wages over this long period, while they seem to reflect great bargaining power, in truth have been the consequence of postwar majority politics, exerted through government policy.[19]

The Problem of Stabilization Policy

From the start of the postwar period, it has been recognized that the goals of lowering unemployment and reducing or eliminating inflation are to some extent conflicting. In the earlier years, the problem was put quite simply as aiming for full employment consistent with stable prices. The theoretical basis for this view lay in the Keynesian model, which presumes that the level of prices would remain stable, despite increasing demand for total output, unless aggregate demand were pushed beyond the point at which the supply curve for output began to turn upward under the influence of short-run diminishing returns (see OS, OS_2 in Fig. 5.11). By contrast, the money wage level would be rigid downward at any output, and would even remain stable upward although real wages were falling as the price level began to rise. Accordingly, the problem of "full employment planning," as it was then called, was to aim for this upward turning point on the output supply curve, because production at that point would be correlated with a unique quantity of employment, and through this, a given minimum supposedly non-

---

19   During 1975-78, the persistence of "stagflation"—high unemployment with high inflation—has given rise to the Humphrey-Javits (later Humphrey-Hawkins) bill, which would commit the government to unrestricted deficit spending until unemployment falls to some target rate, now 4 percent.

inflationary rate of unemployment. In those times, 3 percent was commonly taken to be that rate.[20]

However, the money wage level and the price level in the actual world failed to behave in the expected fashion. Thus the continuing quest for full employment, which by now had become a political imperative, unfortunately got entangled with price and wage inflation together, not only in the United States but in much of Western Europe as well. In this context, the opinion began to be voiced among some economists that trade unionism, or oligopolistic big business, or both together, had made the attainment of noninflationary full employment impossible.[21] By the end of the 1950s it began to be argued that there existed a series of alternative "trade-offs" for economic policy among given rates of price inflation and associated rates of unemployment. This relationship was supposedly stable and could be expressed geometrically by a Phillips curve, shown in Fig. 5.12 [15, pp. 283-299]. To avoid price inflation, the general rate of unemployment can be brought no lower than X_0, which might well be as high as 10 percent of the labor force. By contrast, if the unemployment rate sought is, say, 5 percent or X_1, then the rate of inflation will be Y_1, or, say, 6 percent.

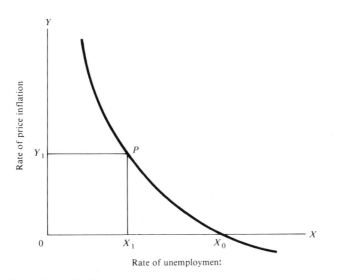

Fig. 5.12 The original Phillips curve.

Within a relatively short time, critics began raising some hard questions: Was the curve itself stable? Was it shaped as depicted? Was it a safe guide to policy, or was some form of direct wage and price controls required as well? Would the "economic actors"—union leaders and business people—behave as the relationship presumes, or in some other way?

In 1968, Friedman dealt the Phillips curve a shattering blow by introducing the concept of a "natural" or long-run rate of general unemployment [7, pp. 1-17; also 5, pp. 456-459]. This rate is indicated by the vertical curve at X_0 in Fig. 5.13. This curve is determined by basic factors in the "real" (nonmonetary) environment; among them, Friedman says, are "the effectiveness of the labor market, the extent of competition or monopoly, the barriers or encouragements to working in various occupations, and so on" [5, p. 458]. Other factors would include the minimum wage and trade union entry rates. Although the natural rate has stability for fairly lengthy periods, it is not fixed for all time. Indeed, it has increased (moved rightward) in recent years for two important reasons. First, the proportion of women, youngsters, and part-time workers has been rising as a percentage of the whole labor force. Because they have above-average mobility they have above-average rates of unemployment, which brings up the natural rate. Second, unemployment compensation, food stamps, and welfare benefits have been increased and made more available. In result the cost of being unemployed has been reduced relative to earnings from taking a job. This, too, raises the rate and volume of "natural" unemployment [5, p. 459; 17, p. 65].

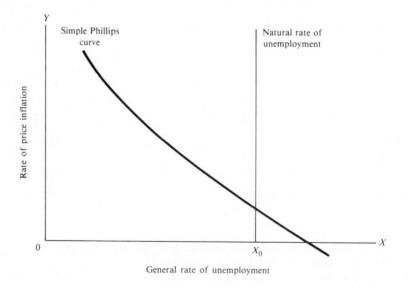

Fig. 5.13 Friedman's natural rate of unemployment.

The connection between the natural rate of unemployment and the nominal or transitory rates observed from month to month can be viewed as the normal or central tendency toward which economic forces are tending to push these transitory rates. Indeed, deviations from the natural rate can occur because economic actors "expect" a general rate of inflation that differs from the actual one. Figure 5.14 indicates in highly simpified fashion how the difference between expected and actual rates actually works. In this diagram X_0 is the natural rate, which is intersected by three different ordinary Phillips curves, each of which is the "perceived" or anticipated average rate of price change.

Start, now, with point A, and suppose that total money demand begins increasing, say, through a larger deficit, incurred in hopes of bringing the unemployment rate down to X_1. Each employer sees the process as creating larger demand and higher prices, and hence falling real wages. His or her incentive will be to increase the number of jobs. Each worker sees the same process as increasing money wages with future average price intact, and hence as a rise in real wages as well. In consequence, labor supply increases at the same time as labor demand from the employers. But this paradoxical situation cannot last: The rate of inflation will move upward from B to C as the rate of unemployment moves down to X_1. The actors accordingly adjust their expectations upward regarding inflation: A new Phillips curve, passing through X_0 at E, replaces the older and lower one at A. But this same upward revision in the expected rate of inflation cancels out both the anticipated fall

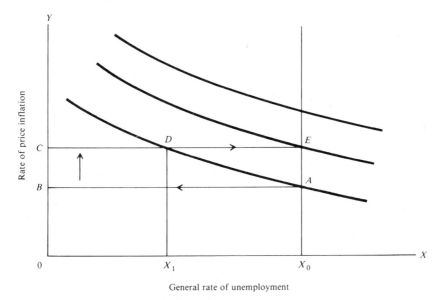

Fig. 5.14   Mechanism of the natural rate of unemployment.

(by employers) and rise (by workers) of real wages. The stimulus for real expansion is lost, and the unemployment rate goes back up to X_0 on the natural rate curve. Point E accordingly becomes the terminal point of the process, because at this point actual and expected rates of inflation are once more in balance, at a higher point on the natural rate curve [5, pp. 456-458].

This abstract but necessary exercise teaches us, first of all, that no stable Phillips curve exists to guide the government policymakers in their choice of targets for unemployment and inflation. Thus the problem of economic stabilization is indeed difficult. Second, the natural rate analysis shows that any long-term reduction of the unemployment rate is a far more complicated matter than the advocates of the now old-fashioned policy "medicine" of bigger deficits and easy money ever contemplated.

Taking the stabilization problem first, as doubts about the Phillips curve began to emerge by the early 1960s, some experts contended that what was required was an "incomes policy" that embraced standards for wage and price changes. In the United States, a highly sophisticated version, without regulation and enforcement machinery, was introduced by the Kennedy administration in January 1962. Four years later, the "guideposts" system had collapsed, in a major strike of airline mechanics. In 1971 the Nixon administration attempted a direct system of wage and price controls that was abandoned within less than two years. Overseas, the British government has attempted several "social contract" schemes to contain upward pressure on wages by the trade unions by giving assurances that the rate of price inflation would be brought down to some designated level. These arrangements, too, have proved less than successful.

One of the central problems for stabilization policy, as Wachter points out, is our lack of precise knowledge of the rate of unemployment that would be noninflationary [17. The noninflationary rate and Friedman's natural rate are similar but not identical.]. Our statistical procedures are not yet good enough, although a strong argument can be made for a rate of 5.5 to 6 percent today. The problem here is that even if we accept this range, political pressures insistently push for 3 to 4 percent. When those pressures are accepted, the natural rate mechanism is likely to come into play, aborting the hoped-for permanent reduction of unemployment, while accelerating the general rate of inflation.

Another aspect of the stabilization problem involves wages, particularly under collective bargaining.[22] One problem in this area is the lag effects of long-term contracts, where annual increases plus cost-of-living adjustments have to be allowed to work themselves out if we are to preserve free collective bargaining. Another difficulty is the inflexibility of wages in the sense that because of long-term contracts, orbits and patterns, and universal downward rigidity, much of the wage system is unresponsive to policy

---

22   For a review of wage stabilization policy in the United States, see Daniel Quinn Mills [14, pp. 3-72].

measures and lacks sensitivity to variations in labor demand. Most of these obstacles to effective stabilization are inherent products of collective bargaining. For good reason, no democratic government is prepared to contemplate substantial interference with bargaining arrangements and institutions [13, pp. 213-229].

The remaining major problem in stabilization policy is unemployment. Clearly, whether one has in mind Friedman's natural rate or its close variant, the noninflationary rate, it would improve the efficiency of the American economy to get both rates down. So stated, the problem cannot be effectively dealt with by the conventional expedient of increasing total demand. Rather, the appropriate solution is to alter those structural factors that have made both rates so high in recent years.

First, because almost half of the current unemployed are under 25 years of age, stress should be directed to overcoming the obstacles to the employment of the young. Among these obstacles are inadequate vocational preparation, an inadequate bridging of the gap between school and work, badly designed entry-level jobs, and an excessively high minimum wage.[23] Second, the unemployment compensation system, food stamps, and welfare tend to *promote* as well as relieve unemployment. They do so by narrowing the spread between take-home wages and compensation or welfare benefits, which reduces the willingness to accept jobs. In addition, food stamps and welfare inflate the numbers of unemployed by the requirement that one must register as available for a job as a condition for eligibility. Finally, if our labor markets were better organized, this would work to reduce both turnover (which shows up as unemployment) and the average duration of periods of unemployment.

REFERENCES

1. Boulding, Kenneth E. *Economic Analysis.* 3d ed. New York: Harper, 1955.

2. Buchanan, James M., and Richard W. Wagner. *Democracy in Deficit: The Political Legacy of Lord Keynes.* New York: Academic Press, 1977.

3. Eckstein, Otto, and Thomas A. Wilson. "The Determination of Money Wages in American Industry." *Quarterly Journal of Economics* 76 (August 1962): 379-414.

4. Fisher, Irving. *The Purchasing Power of Money: Its Determination and Relation to Credit, Interest and Crises.* Assisted by Harry G. Brown. New York: Macmillan, 1911.

5. Friedman, Milton. "Nobel Lecture: Inflation and Unemployment." *Journal of Political Economy* 85 (June 1977): 3.

6. ———. *Price Theory: A Provisional Text.* Chicago: Aldine, 1962.

---

23   This rate was raised from $2.30 to $2.65 hourly in 1977 and is scheduled to rise to $3.35 by 1981.

7. ———. "The Role of Monetary Policy." *American Economic Review* 83 (March 1968): 1.

8. Gordon, Robert Aaron. *Business Fluctuations.* 2d ed. New York: Harper, 1961.

9. Hicks, J.R. *The Theory of Wages.* London: Macmillan & Co., 1935.

10. Levinson, Harold M. "Unionism, Concentration, and Wage Changes: Toward a Unified Theory." *Industrial and Labor Relations Review* (20 January 1967): 2.

11. Lewis, H.G. *Unionism and Relative Wages in the United States: An Empirical Inquiry.* Chicago: University of Chicago Press, 1963.

12. Marshall, Alfred. *Principles of Economics: An Introductory Volume.* 8th ed. London: Macmillan & Co., 1930.

13. Mills, Daniel Quinn. *Government, Labor, and Inflation: Wage Stabilization in the United States.* Chicago: University of Chicago Press, 1975.

14. *NLRB* v. *Denver Building and Construction Trades Council,* 341 U.S. 675 (1951). Cf. Charles O. Gregory, *Labor and the Law,* 2d ed. (New York: W.W. Norton, 1961), pp. 422-423.

15. Phillips, A.W. "The Relationship between Unemployment and the Rate of Change of Money Wages Rates in the United Kingdom, 1861-1957." *Economica* (November 1958): 283-299.

16. Ulman, Lloyd. "Marshall and Friedman on Union Strength." *Review of Economics and Statistics* 37, No. 4 (November 1955): 384-404.

17. Wachter, Michael L. "Some Problems in Wage Stabilization." *American Economic Review* 66, No. 2 (May 1976).

18. ———. "The Wage Process: An Analysis of the Early 1970s." *Brookings Papers on Economic Activity* 2 (1974).

19. Webb, Sidney, and Beatrice Webb. *Industrial Democracy.* 1920 edition. New York: Augustus M. Kelley, 1965, pp. 279-323.

Some 6
Unsettled Questions
Involving Unionism:
Collective Bargaining
in the
Public Sector

In this chapter we shall examine at length some aspects of American unionism posing important issues that remain unsettled, both in professional opinion and in public policy. The first one concerns the nature of unionism in the public sector. In particular, are union-employer relations in the government domain simply a replica of collective bargaining in the private sector, or are they more accurately to be viewed as an extension of politics and political power?

TYPES OF GOVERNMENT UNIONS

It is probably safe to say that although diversity has always been a ruling characteristic of American unionism, it is nowhere more evident than in the public sector, where it involves the organizations themselves, their structures, and their methods of advancing their interests.[1]

For a start, it is necessary to distinguish *associations* from *unions* of public employees. In part the difference may reflect the desire of the group to emphasize its professional status and interests, and in some cases even its hostility to unionism and collective bargaining. The Fraternal Order of Police falls into this category, but in the interests of accuracy it also should be noted that there are three other police organizations, all of which have very different outlooks from the Fraternal Order of Police. In addition, there are other associations that do not shy from negotiating on behalf of their members, but prefer not to have explicit identification with the labor movement, even unto refusing to use the terms "collective bargaining" and

---

1   I have relied upon the following sources for this section: Jack Steiber [5]; Harry H. Wellington and Ralph K. Winter, Jr. [8]; Hervey A. Juris and Peter Feuille [4]; and Robert E. Doherty [1].

"strike." Within this category, the leading example would be the National Education Association (NEA), which prefers "collective negotiations" and "sanctions." Then there are bodies such as the American Nurses' Association, an organization that combines a broad array of professional interests and concerns with an explicit commitment to collective bargaining that is of over thirty years' standing [5, pp. 10-11]. And finally, there are numerous state and local associations of civil service employees, typically formed initially to promote the merit system and pension and insurance plans. Some of them concentrate upon legislative lobbying exclusively, while others, as in the state of New York, have adopted collective bargaining as well.

There are two principal types of unions of public employees. One is the "pure" government union, whose jurisdiction and membership are entirely in the public sector. A prominent example of this kind of organization is the American Federation of State, County, and Municipal Employees (AFSCME), AFL-CIO, whose base is in state and local government, and which currently is the largest union in the federation. A counterpart type of union at the federal level is the American Federation of Government Employees (AFGE), AFL-CIO. Both the AFSCME and the AFGE accept all occupations within their domains, and hence can be called "industrial" unions. By contrast, there are other purely government-employee unions whose membership base lies in a particular occupation. Within this category should be included the American Federation of Teachers (AFT), AFL-CIO, which competes aggressively with the NEA for members and recognition.[2] Last, there is the International Association of Fire Fighters (IAFF), AFL-CIO, an interesting organization that had ruled out collective bargaining and strikes in the early years after its founding in 1918, but in 1968 removed its self-imposed strike ban and thereby reinforced its commitment to bargaining as its preferred method of achieving change.

The second type of labor organization in the government field is the "mixed" union, in which the membership base lies both in the public and private sectors. Here again the variety is extensive. Two large organizations of this type, both with substantial government components, are the Service Employees International Union (SEIU), AFL-CIO, formerly known as the Building Service Employees, and the Laborers' International Union of North America, AFL-CIO. Other important national unions of similar type are those that represent blue-collar craftsmen in Navy yards, arsenals, the Tennessee Valley Authority, and various research and testing installations. Prominent in this group is the International Association of Machinists, AFL-CIO, and the International Brotherhood of Electrical Workers, AFL-CIO. In both of these cases, the primary membership is to be found in the private sector, while the government component is more likely to have its wages and working conditions set not through bargaining but by comparative surveys

---

2   In 1972, the AFT and the NEA actually attempted a merger in New York State, but the effort had failed by 1976.

of the occupation in the adjacent private sector (the so-called "prevailing wages" technique).

If, to get an order of magnitude, we combine the membership figures for the government unions and associations, the total was about 5.3 million in 1974, when there were 14.3 million government employees. Roughly speaking, then, between 30 and 40 percent of all public workers belonged to unions [7, *passim*]. Since 1960, employment in government has increased more rapidly than in the private sector, and most of the increase has occurred at the state and local level.

VARIATIONS IN METHODS OF PROMOTING INTERESTS

In popular belief unionism is automatically associated with collective bargaining. However, this relationship does not hold for the public sector. Indeed, collective bargaining as such is a relatively late arrival, although it has now become the dominant technique for promoting membership interests.

To illustrate, the mixed unions in government have been considerably less concerned about bargaining and the right to strike or about legislation to provide an accompanying apparatus for unit determinations, representation elections, and awards of recognition [5, pp. 119-120, 175-176]. Instead they have pursued their objectives with quiet success for many years by endorsing and supporting candidates for office, by lobbying and the exertion of political influence, and by sustained pressure for favorable legislation.

Without doubt, one of the great exemplars of this approach was the postal unions, who used it with the Congress during the years that the Post Office was a cabinet department rather than a public corporation. Another interesting variant, made prominent many years ago in San Francisco, involved the drafting of amendments to the city charter favorable to the unions of city employees—amendments that usually were assured of adoption at the polls in this highly pro-union city. By this method, the municipal transit union won an amendment many years ago that required automatic annual wage increases under a formula that linked wages to the average of those in the highest-paying cities in the industry—a variant of the prevailing wages technique.

On the whole, these alternatives to collective bargaining rest upon the ability to bring pressure upon a lawmaking body to provide higher wages and benefits, or upon direct appeals to the voters to sanction such gains by mandate.

There is no reason to expect that these forms of political bargaining will ultimately be replaced by the collective type found in private industry. Yet it is true that with the help of new state laws, Presidential Executive Orders for the Federal Civil Service, municipal ordinances, and court decisions establishing the right to collective bargaining in several jurisdictions, collective bargaining has become the most prominent technique today.

DIVERSITY IN BARGAINING UNITS

With the spread of collective bargaining, a diverse array of bargaining units has emerged. In major part these different units have tended to reflect the jurisdictional interests of the several employee organizations involved.

To illustrate, the police and fire associations have sought representation rights that embrace the key occupations occupied by their members. In education, the NEA and the AFT have followed essentially the same principle by confining their interest to teachers and closely related support personnel, such as counselors and guidance teachers, while excluding school bus drivers and building service employees. In this connection, one development of particular interest has been the gradual shift since 1960 of the NEA through which managerial personnel such as superintendents and principals have been excluded from unit coverage. Over its century-long preceding history, the NEA had always emphasized that it was an organization of professionals in the service of education as such, and hence was not concerned with the adversary interests of teachers as employees. With the growing militancy of teachers in recent years, together with intensifying competition from the AFT, the NEA has gradually come to embrace the role of bargaining agent. In consequence, the managerial groups have had to go.

The mixed unions have displayed a measure of organizational opportunism in matters concerning bargaining units. Thus the Teamsters have concentrated on street and highway maintenance departments and sanitation departments where they compete with the Laborers' International Union for recognition in many cases.[3] Proceeding in somewhat different fashion, the SEIU has found much of its organizational base among service personnel in hospitals and schools and social service employees [5, pp. 4-5, 141].

Among the purely government unions, the AFSCME has displayed a propensity for all-inclusive units of a city- and countywide type—in a sense "residual" or catch-all units that absorb all employees except those in particular occupations such as teaching, uniformed services, and transit operating and maintenance [5, p. 139]. Indeed, this very flexibility, together with the target groups involved, accounts for the union's phenomenal growth over the past decade.

One final observation concerns the scope of urban bargaining units. As already noted, the general practice has been to establish occupational units for education, uniformed protective services, and transit. For the very substantial remaining group of employees, two alternatives have emerged. One is the large inclusive unit of the type developed in Philadelphia. The other is fragmentation into many jurisdictions, more as the consequence of political power coupled to union ambitions, as in New York City, than of any

---

3   The Laborers have their main jurisdictional base in the building trades.

overall design. The Philadelphia approach makes the task of bargaining much easier for management because it avoids the "Balkanization" of bargaining units. By contrast, the New York City pattern has fostered interunion rivalries, "leapfrog" tactics, and endless negotiating and jurisdictional problems. However, the price to be paid for the one big unit is the danger of a massive strike. If city management is well unified and not subordinate to the political influence of the unions, it may be more effective in behalf of the taxpayers and users of city services to have a Balkanized system of units [8, pp. 45, 102]. However, this has not been the case in New York City, in large part because of weakness and failure on the management side [3]. Aside from this special element, the fragmented unit system, even if inconvenient to both management and the union, at least does allow basic differences in interests among employee groups to be expressed.

Turning now to the federal government, the principal bargaining units involve the civil service employees. They typically are broken up by department and agency. However, Congress has reserved the vital matters of pay and fringe benefits for legislative action, which has kept the federal unions with relatively little to bargain about. Their principal concern has been the development of and coadministration of a grievance and advisory arbitration procedure. Thus federal labor relations involve a dual structure, with the Civil Service Commission in control of the vital matters of pay and fringe benefits by means of legislative sanctions, while the civil service unions are largely confined to issues of personnel administration.

LINES OF ACTION IN COLLECTIVE BARGAINING

Diversity asserts itself once again as regards the manner in which the government unions have pressed their cause in collective bargaining. Here it should be noted first that the strike is outlawed for the federal civil service as well as in certain state and local jurisdictions. Where such is the case, strikes are not necessarily eliminated: they are simply made illegal. Their occurrence or nonoccurrence then depends upon other considerations.

In the bargaining process before stalemate or *impasse* is reached, the public-worker unions and associations usually enjoy an advantage over their counterparts in the private sector: namely, the ability to exert political influence and even on occasion to divide the ranks of management. Politicians seek votes: there are no profits to maximize, and accordingly, the profit motive does not operate as a magnetic force to unify management against its union adversary [2, pp. 131-133]. What actually matters in these situations is the strength or weakness of unionism in the political jurisdiction in question. In states such as New York and California, and in cities such as New York City and San Francisco, the power of organized labor is so great that it is relatively easy to bend the legislature or the city council in a favorable direction, regardless of costs to the taxpayers or the quality of the public service to its users.

The most direct method for doing this is through control of a political machine itself. This makes possible a "deal" and opens the way to a type of political theater—strikes, threats, strident claims and charges—whose real function is to prepare public opinion for acceptance and to distribute the blame for any adverse results. If the machine is not primarily based upon organized labor, then divide-and-conquer tactics may be employed. A crisis is built up, its dire implications are emphasized, and an effort is made to isolate a recalcitrant mayor or faction in the council by rallying a majority opposition. One version of this happened at the beginning of Mayor Lindsay's term in January 1966, when the Transport Workers Union shut down all public transportation in New York City. At the outset the mayor struck a pose of righteous opposition in the spirit of the traditional municipal reformer who will make no deals with "the interests." An injunction was obtained but promptly violated, and the leader of the Transport Workers Union was then put in jail. The pressure then began to build against the mayor. Within two weeks he surrendered, granting the union an increase of double anything it had ever gained before [3, pp. 80-81]. Lindsay experienced another version of this strategy in a garbage strike a little over a year later, when the union managed to separate Governor Rockefeller from the mayor, using the governor to extract a settlement more generous than Lindsay was prepared to accept.

The application of political power by organizations of government employees often has been most conveniently accomplished by means of the strike, a weapon that has been widely used, even where it is illegal. It has been most effective where the service affected is vital to the peoples' daily lives—for example, fire and police protection, garbage collection, transit, and public education. These services generally tend to be organized by an occupationally based union or association such as the NEA, the AFT, the Fire Fighters, or the various police unions, rather than by catchall organizations such as the AFSCME or the SEIU. By extending their jurisdictions so broadly, these latter unions have incurred a double disadvantage: If they strike over their entire unit, they create an indiscriminate citywide crisis that is likely to bring prompt intervention, while if they attempt to strike selectively they must shut down relatively unimportant services, which lessens the pressure they can bring to bear.

This suggests an important conclusion: The occupational form of public-employee organization may be viewed as the counterpart of the traditional craft union in the private sector. Its strength rests upon the importance of the service, the relative unimportance of its wage or salary bill to the total budget, and the peculiar cohesion that the members of an occupational union typically display when they strike and come under counterattack.

A few illustrations will demonstrate the point. One certainly would have to be the transit strike in New York City in early 1966, which ended in capitulation by Mayor Lindsay, apparently on terms much more favorable than the union ever actually had hoped to obtain. Another example occurred in San Francisco in the summer of 1975, when the police began an unusual job-action tactic by issuing hundreds of tags for parking violations. The union then followed with an actual strike. A thoroughly angry board of supervisors voted not to increase its original offer, backed by an equally angry public. Within hours, Mayor Alioto found it to his political advantage to employ a little-known section of the city charter that enabled him to settle the strike on the union's terms, amidst overwhelming popular disgust.

A final instance involves the firemen's union in Dayton, Ohio, in the summer of 1977. Here again an *impasse* in negotiations ended in a strike in which several buildings were allowed to burn to the ground, despite the efforts of volunteers to put the fires out. In the end, the mayor and city council surrendered to the union's terms, despite considerable public indignation over the strike.

The enumeration of these various union successes may prove unintentionally misleading, by suggesting irresistible power. In fact, a shift in the balance of political power has been taking place in recent years, while the big gains won by public-sector unionism were largely over by 1972. In part, of course, this may reflect the old principle that new unionism quickly establishes wage premiums, while old unions strive to protect them. But there is more to the matter than this. A public revolt against high taxes has been building gradually but extensively for some five years, of which the passage of the Proposition 13 initiative in California is simply a prominent example.[4] School budgets and school bond issues have been defeated, tax limitation amendments have been introduced in several states, and Congress itself has begun to take a serious interest in cutting taxes.

PECULIARITIES OF THE PUBLIC SECTOR

The first major difference from the private sector is that the services produced by government typically are provided free of charge. Thus there is no loss of revenue from a strike, and this lowers the cost to management of disagreeing with the union. At the same time, since the production of government services is subsidized by funding from a central source whose own revenues are supplied mostly by taxpayers, managers of government activities are not under the constant whiplash of profit-and-loss. Thus they have more discretion than their private-sector counterparts. True, their budgets impose constraints, but they have no obligation to maximize profits. Indeed, at the state and local levels, even the budget constraint is often made flexible by the availability of emergency funds, and by revenue sharing and categorical grants from the federal government. In consequence, the incentive of management to resist has to be weaker than in private enterprise, where the venture is fully accountable and has to be self-liquidating.

---

4   This constitutional amendment set a low maximum limit for the percentage rate of tax upon the assessed valuation of privately owned property.

A second difference is the monopolistic character of most government services. Each of them, in fact, is surrounded by a gap in the chain of substitutes, at least in the short run and for most users. To be sure, some degree of consumer substitution is possible—one can walk or drive instead of using public transportation. Parents can put their children in private schools, while private police and fire protection can be purchased by those who can afford it. One can also put off a visit to the zoo and read a book instead. And over the longer run, people can and do move from municipalities and even states whose public services are costly, irregular, or poor in quality.

Thus there is some elasticity of demand for the various services of government, and, as Alfred Marshall pointed out long ago for the private sector, elasticity is greater in the long run than it is in the short, because more time is available to allow consumers to adapt. But for the ordinary citizen elasticity is nevertheless quite low at all times for the more important services.

The third difference—the obscure status of the public "employer" and the difficulty of achieving adequate bargaining in management's behalf—is the most important of them all. In order to bargain effectively, a manager must have the authority to make an agreement. Even more, that authority must be integral: there must be no possibility of undermining it. If these absolutely essential requirements are met, then management can act effectively to protect the taxpayers and the users of the service in negotiating with the union.

This leads to the final difference from the private sector, and it is a difference inherent to democratic government itself. It is that in almost all jurisdictions the lawmaking and the management functions are separate. In others words, the managers of departments, bureaus, and agencies depend for their funds upon budgets enacted by legislatures, city councils, county boards of supervisors, and boards of education.

This dual structure of power lacks the internal cohesion that the profit-and-loss mechanism imposes upon the typical private enterprise. In consequence, even in a purely technical sense, effective collective bargaining in the public sector requires a delicate coordination of arrangements and of outlook between the lawmakers on the one side and the management negotiators on the other. At a much more mundane level, the critical problem is, How can the public employer keep the union from dividing his already tenuously united ranks? For if splitting can be accomplished, management is certain to fail. And when it fails, sacrifice of the interests of the users of the service and of the taxpayers necessarily follows. Where this occurs—and it often does—the real bargaining becomes political and has no parallel with the adversary system in the private sector. Put another way, the social utility of the manager's adversary role is destroyed because there is a decisive political advantage to someone in allowing the union to dominate both sides of the bargaining table.

Beyond question, then, managerial cohesion is one of the central problems for genuine collective bargaining in the public sector, not the strike and not the technical issue of the sovereignty of government.

If adequate unity and accountability of public management are to be achieved, the illusion must be shed that collective bargaining is a task to be assigned to the experts—negotiators, mediators, fact finders, and arbitrators. In fact, the only conceivable way to protect the public interest in the cost and quality of government services is to make the key elected officials openly responsible—in the double sense of formulating a bargaining position for management that is fully reflective of the public interest and of accepting accountability at the polls for the consequence of settlements actually reached. Certainly labor-relations experts can be helpful and even essential in a staff capacity. But for effective bargaining on the side of public management, the mayor, the governor, or the chairman of a board of education must have his or her budget officers at hand throughout the process.

As Raymond Horton [3] has shown very forcefully for New York City, the collapse of the management position in that community was effected by a conscious decision by the potentially influential elected officials to extricate themselves from responsibility for labor relations—by a transfer of power to experts in the Office of Collective Bargaining. Shortly thereafter, a tripartite system of binding compulsory arbitration of unresolved disputes was established. Through this delegation of responsibility, the elected officials sacrificed political power for city management, at the same time handing over the negotiating task to experts whose expertise unfortunately did not include detailed substantive knowledge of management's problems and interests. In the same process, the top officials shed all accountability for the public impact of the bargains reached. Indeed, the ultimate absurdity was the tripartite arbitration panel, in which the city and the union were placed in equal positions regarding matters of critical importance to the public interest.

Avoidance of these mistakes, of course, does not mean that the chief elected officials and their budget officers would never allow "politics" to intrude into negotiations or settlements. But it would preserve the principle of accountability in democratic government, it would allow management concerns to be expressed at the bargaining table, and it would permit public opinion to exert its proper role.[5] But beyond this prospect we cannot go. Any state or community possesses a pluralism of competing interests. Inevitably, the result is "politics." It would be utopian to look for ways to establish a "nonpolitical" system of bargaining institutions in government. The best that one can hope for is an arrangement that provides a direct link

---

5   The role of aroused public opinion need not be fanciful, as the municipal unions in San Francisco found out in 1975.

of accountability from the bargainers to the voters, with enough "daylight" in the negotiations to hold in check the possibility for secret deals. In highly unionized communities, politics may continue to favor the civil servants and their unions over the consumers and the taxpayers, although the growing taxpayers' revolt makes this less certain. But in any event more restraint on behalf of management and the public interest will become possible than where the elected officials abdicate their responsibilities by delegating them to professionals whose chief concern is limited to conflict resolution.

STRIKES IN THE PUBLIC SECTOR

The discussion above brings us to the problem of strikes in the public sector. At the one extreme, there is the traditional view that there can be no right to strike against government, anywhere and at any time. At the other, there is the view that at bottom there is no real difference between the public and the private sectors, from which it supposedly follows that any limitation on the right to strike in either domain should be based only on a showing of a clear and direct threat to the public health and safety.

The traditional ground for a ban against all public-service strikes has been the doctrine of sovereignty, that is, the notion that the power of government is absolute and supreme, and therefore not negotiable. Time has brought about a reformulation of the doctrine, in the proposition that it would be an illegal delegation of power for government to share its power with others, for example, with a labor union through negotiation and administration of a collective agreement [8, pp. 36-40]. So stated, this principle is not very persuasive when applied to the many routine cases of government collective bargaining. However, its real interest is less as an objection to a technical sharing of power, as compared to a unilateral prescription of pay, benefits, and rules through a civil service statute or ordinance. Rather, it is that bargaining in the public service brings into being a set of new interest groups—unions or associations—whose power will soon become substantial. The natural consequence, in turn, will be to bend the distribution of income excessively in favor of civil servants at the expense of the whole public, and to provide these unions with "too powerful a lever in municipal decision-making" [8, pp. 26-29].

In other words, the argument runs, the formation of these new interest groups puts at some risk the pluralistic balance upon which democratic government ultimately depends.[6] Seriously viewed, this reasoning suggests that we ought not to extend public-sector collective bargaining any further, or at least should seek to contain it by imposing limits on the scope of agreements or by subjecting the monetary aspects of settlements to public referenda.

Whatever view one adopts toward the whole problem, it should now be obvious that the question of strikes in the public sector is not the heart of the

---

6   For another version of the argument, see [6].

controversy over public-sector bargaining, but actually is a decidedly secondary issue. Yet it must be faced, for even the most unreserved advocates of government collective bargaining concede the necessity for some strike control where health and safety may be at stake.

As against a universal ban, there is much merit in a more selective approach. Not all strikes against government are necessarily against the public interest in any significant degree. In fact, if one holds the contrary, then the urge becomes irresistible to adopt the uncritical policy of labor peace at all costs [3, pp. 130-131]. But labor relations are not a zero-sum game that always pits the civil servants against the public, and it is not an imperative that all public services must be kept going without interruption. Indeed, the appeasement syndrome in these matters has many consequences, all of them adverse. It fosters a "hang the costs" notion—settle at any price. The danger is that this would build up the unions and encourage them to resort to more and more extremist strategies. And it fosters excessive reliance upon peacekeeping machinery in the hands of neutrals who have neither the knowledge of budgets, nor the responsibility for management, nor the accountability to the voters to justify such a tender of trust.

Now, to address the problem of selective strike control itself, the critical question is what to do after *impasse* is reached. The next step might be fact finding with recommendations, then further mediation; if these fail, the authorities could apply for an injunction upon grounds of irreparable impending damage to the community. At the same time, the whole dispute could be remanded to the lawmaking body for final action. Or, alternatively to this last step, a public referendum might be conducted on that body's final offer. As another alternative, there is the possibility of committing difficult "emergency" strike disputes to compulsory and binding arbitration, as New York City provided in 1972.

The compulsory arbitration approach has much against it and not much to recommend it. It constitutes an open invitation to adventurist and extremist strategies from the outset of negotiations, and through such it defeats the very practice of collective bargaining. It allows the chief public officials to abdicate their responsibilities to a panel of *ad hoc* neutrals, or a single neutral, who in any case cannot be held accountable to the electorate. Thus the link between the voters and their elected representatives is severed and a basic principle of democratic government abandoned.

However, there exist some cases when this technique has worked out without serious adverse results, and in consequence some experts see a limited place for compulsory arbitration. But if the technique is to be applied to issues as basic as pensions and work rules, then the award of the arbitration should be subject to approval by public referendum.

A final basic question involving the public sector concerns strikes in violation of the law or of court orders. In New York State, for example, the former Condon-Wadlin law called for jailing of union leaders and forfeiture of civil service rights of participants. The difficulty with this approach is that it makes martyrs out of the offenders and also loses credibility as a deterrent because it becomes too tempting for politicians to dodge enforcement of the law, particularly in communities where unionism is strong. A more effective alternative would be to concentrate the penalties upon the organization itself. This can be done by a mandatory statutory provision that any union or association that undertakes an illegal strike shall automatically lose its recognition rights for at least two years and will also lose all payments from the public agency for dues withheld from employees.

In concluding this brief consideration of bargaining in the public sector, the point should be emphasized that no matter what form it takes, the political factor is ever-present in some way. In some situations, to be sure, it may be possible to simulate quite closely the private-sector counterpart, provided that the fundamental problem of unity of management can be solved. But it is politics that makes the problem so fundamental and so pervasive. And it is politics that intrudes as a special factor at every stage in public-sector disputes. Thus it seems more accurate to term the entire process *political* rather than *collective* bargaining, to emphasize the differences from rather than the similarities to the private-sector system of negotiation. Market forces still have some role to play, but it is political decisions that are the more decisive to the outcome.

REFERENCES

1 Doherty, Robert E. Unpublished manuscript on bargaining in education, to be published in a forthcoming volume entitled *Collective Bargaining: Contemporary American Experience,* prepared under auspices of Industrial Relations Research Association.

2 Hildebrand, George H. "The Public Sector." In *Frontiers of Collective Bargaining,* edited by John T. Dunlop and Neil W. Chamberlain. New York: Harper and Row, 1967.

3 Horton, Raymond D. *Municipal Labor Relations in New York City: Lessons of the Lindsay-Wagner Years.* New York: Praeger, 1973.

4. Juris, Hervey A., and Peter Feuille. *Police Unionism: Power and Impact in Public Sector Bargaining.* Lexington, MA: D.C. Heath, 1973.

5. Stieber, Jack. *Public Employee Unionism: Structure, Growth, Policy.* Washington, D.C.: The Brookings Institution, 1971.

6. Summers, Robert S. *Collective Bargaining and Public Benefit Conferral: A Jurisprudential Critique.* Institute of Public Employment. New York State School of Industrial and Labor Relations, Cornell University. Ithaca, NY: Cornell University, 1976.

7. U.S. Department of Commerce. *Statistical Abstract of the United States 1975.* 96th annual edition. Washington, D.C.: Government Printing Office, 1975.

8. Wellington, Harry H., and Ralph K. Winter, Jr. *The Unions and the Cities.* Washington, D.C.: The Brookings Institution, 1971.

THE NATURE OF CATEGORICAL DISCRIMINATION

To most people today, the word "discrimination" has an invidious conno-
tation and rightly so, although the reasons are complex. In the neutral sense,
discrimination refers simply to the act of making careful and accurate
distinctions in one's judgments. But when a person is charged with discriminatory beliefs or actions, the implication is that he or she is moved by
prejudice regarding whatever distinction is at issue. And what is at issue here
is the act of ascribing to an individual certain traits or stereotypes commonly
attributed to some group with which the individual may readily be identified.
More important, the act of judgment in some given context of this sort is not
based upon the merits of the person so judged, but rather is grounded upon
an arbitrary group of traits taken to be characteristic of the category of
which he or she is a member. This is the essential meaning of *categorical discrimination.* It must also be borne in mind that from the standpoint of the
one making the judgment, the traits so assigned may be looked upon either
favorably or unfavorably, although naturally it is the negative side that
commands most attention and concern today.

For present purposes, categorical discrimination is employed most
commonly with respect to a person's race, sex, or ethnicity. In each instance
there are physical or cultural characteristics that make identification of
individual persons by category relatively easy. What is central is that, once
identification is made, the entire cluster of customary beliefs and opinions
about the category as a whole is then ascribed to the individual as well. This
transfer of the outsider's perception of the group to any one of its members
is what is meant by *prejudice,* because a preconceived judgment is involved
that ascribes status, and, through this, prescribes a systematic mode of
conduct and attitude toward this individual. In the usual case, personal
achievements or even the opportunity to demonstrate one's own qualities

are not what matter. Ascribed status, not actual or potential accomplishments, is what counts. Indeed, if the ascribed characteristics are viewed negatively and the power exists to enforce that view, the basis will exist for the automatic exclusion of any member of the group from freely competitive opportunities through which actual merit and potential could be demonstrated and assessed. In the extreme case, almost complete segregation of the group from the remainder of society may be effected.

It goes without saying that categorical discrimination as just described long ago found expression in labor markets, among employers and employees, and within some unions. Illustrations are countless. In the 1870s there were riots against the Chinese whose labor had just made possible the completion of the Pacific railroad. For decades many of the mining companies of the West refused to allow Spanish-speaking workers to rise above common-labor jobs. In factories around the country, "female" jobs have long been common. And in the old firemen's union on the railroads, for decades there existed a constitutional clause barring blacks from membership. Then there was the old patrimonial tradition of some labor organizations by which admission was limited to the sons and nephews (but not the daughters!) of members. All of these are cases of categorical discrimination at work long ago. As we shall see, there are modern cases as well.

To grasp the problem in its full complexity and thereby help to resolve it in the labor-management field, it is essential to understand the customs, practices, rules, and mechanisms through which such discrimination and its most extreme variant, segregation, became institutionalized by management and unions.

Besides the institutional approach we have just considered, there is also the work of economists in developing a theory of discrimination based upon the principles of choice and maximization of utility. As Ronald Oaxaca has put the matter, the economist views human behavior as goal directed or purposive [15, p. 2]. Thus discrimination in the labor market is viewed as a calculated act with putatively predictable consequences in the large as regards, for example, differentials in wage rates and earnings, conditions of employment, and so on.

This line of analysis found modern expression two decades ago in the work of Gary Becker [3]. Becker treats discrimination as a "taste" possessed by some employers and workers, in the sense that such a person will pay a money price to avoid transactions with the members of the group discriminated against. Given some highly abstract and restrictive assumptions, Becker's model suggests that some employers will sacrifice profits to avoid hiring blacks, while some workers will accept lower wages to avoid working with them.

A somewhat different attack on the problem is to account for the profits of discrimination by looking at the ways in which job segregation, for example, in "female" or "Mexican" occupations, makes possible positively but steeply sloped supply curves for these types of workers. In turn this permits the employer to engage in monopsonistic discrimination, in the sense that by setting employment at the point at which marginal wage outlay equals marginal value product, the employer can extract a monopsony profit, bringing about an adverse wage differential to the group as well [15, pp. 11-19; for another account of the economics of the matter, 1, pp. 3-33].

For certain technical reasons, the approach to categorical discrimination through conventional technical economics tends to concentrate mainly upon employers and to some extent individual employees and to pay relatively little attention to labor unions and institutional practices. However, unionism is the central concern of this book. Accordingly, our next task is to examine the role of the unions in the problem of discrimination.

CATEGORICAL DISCRIMINATION INVOLVING UNIONS

Discrimination according to race and sex has a long history in American unionism. However, it is a mixed history in several senses.[1] Thus the Knights of Labor had an "ideal of solidarity irrespective of race"—an ideal that the AFL abandoned after its first few years because it was a barrier to its expansion.

Moreover, most unions do not have *officially* sanctioned discriminatory policies, although a few do. Further, in some cases the practice has been overt, while in others it has been covert. Then, too, there have been organizations whose records have been clean throughout.

Considerable diversity has been shown in the mechanisms through which discrimination has been effected. In good part, these differences in mechanisms have been cross-linked to the types of unions involved. For example, craft unions—now sometimes called "referral unions" because they act as intermediaries, operate hiring halls where idle members register for jobs and through which employers request workers [4, p. 105; also 6, p. 126]. By control of referrals, such unions exert strategic control over entry into the trade. Thus in such situations discrimination is likely to begin at this point. By contrast, the industrial, "factory" and mixed occupational unions normally provide no referrals, meaning in practical terms that the employer is free to hire at the gate or in any manner he or she wishes. Union policies and practices having either discriminatory intent or effect accordingly will assert themselves in these cases only *after* entry into employment and completion of the probationary period, in particular through contractually provided seniority and transfer systems along with other joint union-management controls over labor flows.

---

1   The pioneer study of discrimination by labor unions is [13], with a foreword by Sumner H. Slichter.

Looking to the past again for a moment, Herbert Northrup found through a careful survey some thirty-five years ago that discriminatory union racial policies could be separated into two categories. In one, the policy was outright exclusion from membership by ritual, by constitutional provision, or by tacit consent. Practically all groups of this type were craft unions, with their predominant base in railroading and construction. Most of these organizations were AFL affiliates, although a substantial number were independent bodies. In the second category were those unions that accorded blacks segregated auxiliary status—that is, "Jim Crow" locals and sections that were usually denied any voice in negotiations or union affairs [13, pp. 2-5].[2] Again, the organizations were predominantly of the craft type. Northrup accordingly reasoned that the exclusion of blacks served the traditional economic purpose of "making labor scarce."

Since enactment of the Civil Rights Act in 1964, of course, all of these discriminatory arrangements and practices have been illegal. But the craft and occupational unions in great part still control admissions to formal apprenticeship programs, admissions to helper jobs through which the employee learns the trade on the job, examinations to determine qualifications for full journeyman status, admission to the union itself, and referrals to job opportunities. Obviously, then, opportunities for open as well as covert discrimination still exist, although technically they are not beyond the reach of the law. In the next section we shall consider some efforts to eliminate this class of discriminatory practices.

We turn at this point to the so-called nonreferral unions to consider the possibilities for discriminatory policies or practices within this group. As regards unions of the industrial or "all jobs" type, one form of discrimination is simply not to organize the members of a minority group at all [4, p. 105].[3] Doubtless this approach is comparatively rare these days, but where it occurs it involves complete exlusion of the members of the minority group from any direct benefit of union representation.

Because industrial unionism bases itself entirely upon the control of labor flows inside the plant and typically has no voice concerning the entry of new workers, the points at which discrimination can occur are also internal to the plant. One method, which has been documented in rubber and tobacco manufacturing, involves the maintenance of separate seniority lists distinguished by race, with preference for whites in promotions and other benefits, where the jobs are identical for both groups. Another version is to employ fictitious differences in the jobs according to race, although there are no substantive differences. In this way, separate lines of

---

2 It should be noted that both the Plasterers and the Bricklayers never had formal exclusionary arrangements.

3 For further discussion of discrimination involving industrial unions, see also [14]; [2, pp. 88-112]; [9, pp. 113-123]; and [7].

progression and seniority districts can be established, to the disadvantage of blacks, women, or some other group.

A second main variant for discrimination is accomplished by means of a common-entry labor pool with promotional ladders open only to the preferred group. This arrangement denies the members of the excluded minority all opportunity to qualify for higher-level jobs and then to acquire the progressive steps in on-the-job training through which skills are acquired and built up.

A third possibility involves three elements, all of which have turned up in the basic steel industry: (1) a departmentalized job structure designed by the employer; (2) a hiring policy that excluded women from the mills, but accepted blacks, who were mainly assigned to a particular group of departments where the work was inherently less desirable because of heat, dust, noise, and lesser safety; and (3) a negotiated system of departmental seniority that could not be used for interdepartment transfers or that forbade such transfers entirely [14, pp. 1264-1266].[4]

Last, there is a subtle form of discrimination that involves neither rules nor institutional arrangements but rather manifests itself in the denial of the right to fair representation in the grievance procedure and arbitration in situations where the grievant is a member of a minority.

At this point it should be acknowledged that other devices have been employed with discriminatory intent over the years, not through the medium of a negotiated seniority system, for example, but at the initiative of the employer with the tacit consent, or even covert pressure, of the incumbent union. The more obvious techniques here involve the requirement of a high-school diploma or the passing of an aptitude test to qualify for employment or promotion. In passing on these requirements, the Supreme Court has taken the position that the employer acquires the burden of proving that they are reasonably related to the jobs involved and therefore constitute a genuine "business necessity." Indeed, where there exists a past history of discriminatory hiring and assignments, and where the failure rate on the tests is significantly greater for the minority employees, then the employer's burden becomes even more exacting to show absence of discriminatory intent (the leading case in this matter is [8]).

IMPACTS OF STATUTORY AND CASE LAW

Reference to *Griggs* v. *Duke Power* brings us directly to consideration of the Civil Rights Act of 1964, which in Title VII regulates the hiring and employment practices of employers, employment agencies, and labor

---

4   Where discrimination in hiring was practiced until, say, 1964, those who were hired (usually whites) inevitably acquired high levels of seniority. If the industry has been stagnant since then, virtually no hiring of minorities is possible unless seniority rights are set aside.

organizations. Viewed as a whole, this statute is an omnibus measure that concerns voting rights, access to public accommodations, access to public facilities, desegregation of public education, nondiscrimination in federally assisted programs, and equal employment opportunity. Over and over again throughout this lengthy measure the target affirmed is the elimination of discrimination or segregation on the basis of "race, color, religion, or national origin."[5]

The principle of equal employment opportunity is another way of saying that in both the search for and occupancy of jobs persons are to be judged by their qualifications and achievements, without regard to characteristics of race or sex. Put a little differently, categorical discrimination is to be purged from the employment relationship—actual or prospective— and all persons are to compete on the basis of equal treatment [5]. However, exception is made where "religion, sex, or national origin is a *bona fide* occupational qualification reasonably necessary to the normal operation" of a business (Sec. 703(e)). In a similar way, Section 703(h) permits "different standards of compensation, or different terms, conditions, or privileges of employment pursuant to a *bona fide* seniority or merit system, or a system which measures earnings by quantity or quality of production, or to employees who work in different locations," provided that none of these differences is the product of an intent to discriminate. In other words, the act does not prescribe literal equality in pay, work, and other working conditions.

The law regulates the employment activities and policies of three groups of organizations in the private sector: employers, employment agencies, and unions, called here labor organizations. Unlawful employment practices of employers include (1) hiring or firing; (2) differentiation in pay, terms, conditions, or privileges of employment; and (3) limiting, segregating, or classifying employees adverse to their employment status—all with respect to discrimination according to race, color, religion, sex, or national origin (Sec. 703(a)). So far as employment agencies are concerned, the prohibitions are directed against referrals or nonreferrals tainted by discriminatory purpose or effect.

This brings us to unlawful practices involving unions: (1) to exclude or expel persons from membership on discriminatory grounds; (2) to limit, segregate, or classify membership (closed admissions, separate seniority lists, "Jim Crow" locals), or to classify or refuse to refer persons to jobs; and (3) to cause or try to cause an employer to discriminate against a person (Sec. 703(c)). In addition, it is an unlawful practice for an employer, a union, or a joint committee to discriminate in the operation of apprenticeship, training, or retraining programs, including on-the-job training— as regards admissions to the program or employment in it (Sec. 703(d)).

---

5 In Title VII, which regulates employment relations, "sex" subsequently has been added as another prohibited category for discrimination.

To enforce the hiring and employment requirements of the law, an Equal Employment Opportunity Commission was created (Sec. 705).[6] Under this provision, either a person claiming injury or a member of the commission itself may bring charges against an employer, employment agency, or labor union. If, after a confidential investigation, the commission finds reasonable cause to accept the truth of the complaint, it will attempt first to resolve the dispute by conciliation and persuasion (Sec. 706(a)). If voluntary settlement cannot be had, the charge can then be lodged formally in a district court of the United States. If the court concludes that an unlawful practice is involved, it may (1) enjoin the action, and (2) order "such affirmative action as may be appropriate" (hiring, reinstatement, possibly back pay to be levied against the offending organization—employer, employment agency, or labor union) (Sec. 706(g)).

Finally, in Section 703(j) a limitation of vital significance has been provided. It reads as follows, in its entirety:

> Nothing contained in this title shall be interpreted to require any employer, employment agency, labor organization, or joint labor-management committee subject to this title or grant preferential treatment to any individual or to any group because of the race, color, religion, sex, or national origin of such individual or group on account of an imbalance which may exist with respect to the total number or percentage of persons of any race, color, religion, sex, or national origin employed by any employer, referred or classified for employment by any employment agency or labor organization, admitted to membership or classified by any labor organization, or admitted to, or employed in, any apprenticeship or other training program, in comparison with the total number or percentage of persons of such race, color, religion, sex, or national origin in any community, state, section, or other area, or in the available work force in any community, State, section, or other area.

On first impression, one would infer that in ruling out categorical discrimination in employment, it was the intent of Congress to prevent *all* such discrimination, whether adverse to one category and favorable to another, and whether malignant or benign in its effects. Certainly this impression comports fully with the underlying purpose of the statute: to provide for equal treatment of all persons in like circumstances, through evaluating them as individuals, without regard to their race, sex, or other category cited in the act.

Section 703(j) thus poses an issue of fundamental juridical, philosophical, and moral import. Was it inserted merely to meet the objections of

---

6   Another mode of regulation, involving employers and unions working on federal contracts, involves the Office of Federal Contract Compliance Programs (OFCCP). Altogether, there are now 18 federal agencies concerned with categorical discrimination.

those members of Congress who feared that the Executive would use the act to reintroduce categorical discrimination to help the members of groups who hitherto had been its victims? Or was this section an explicit declaration of principle, that is, equal opportunity for all, with competition for jobs and promotions to rest only upon comparative judgments of individual merits, without regard to race or other categories?

The bearing of this section has yet to be resolved by the courts. Between 1970 and 1974, for example, the federal courts of appeal in the second, sixth, and ninth circuits have held that preferential quotas are an acceptable remedy despite Section 703(j) in situations in which an employer's numerical disproportions have been found to be the product of unlawful discrimination, and where the remedial quota is appropriate to the scope of the offense [11, pp. 59, 59 n. 81]. Even the decision of the Supreme Court in 1978 in the *Bakke* case leaves the issue unresolved. In consequence, there is a long line of similar cases still to be decided.

One of the critical points of impact of Title VII involves hiring. Hiring is, obviously, the initial point for systematic discrimination. Furthermore, it may involve both employer and union. And finally, hiring occurs both in industries dominated by referral unions, such as construction, and in the noncraft industries where the unions typically are of nonreferral variety.

Because certain of the building trades unions long have had few or no members of the prominent minority groups, the Department of Labor under Secretary W. Willard Wirtz attempted in 1967 to introduce an affirmative action plan in Philadelphia that would open up training and employment opportunities particularly for blacks in that area on construction projects financed with federal funds. Ultimately this plan was found to be illegal because it set aside competitive bidding [6, pp. 130-131]. Then, in September 1969, Secretary of Labor George P. Shultz introduced a second attempt, in which "goals" were set for six skilled trades for the hiring of blacks in a "good-faith" effort, to be guided by "timetables" to monitor progress. This particular "Philadelphia Plan" contained no provisions for recruitment or training of minority workers. Nor did it deal with the vital issue of assured admission of successful applicants into the unions involved [6, pp. 131].

Similar "hometown" plans were negotiated at the behest of the department for other cities, but again without marked success. Thus the later history of Title VII and of Executive Order 11246 in construction has centered upon actions in court rather than "plans" negotiated by relatively powerless umbrella organizations.

When we turn to hiring in the noncraft industries, we can say that the initial effects of Title VII were to push employers, in some cases rather hastily, toward the formulation of "neutral" criteria, that is to say, criteria untainted by discriminatory intent. But, as Lopatka [11, pp. 32-48] points out in his thorough discussion of the *Griggs* case [8], by 1971 neutral standards were no longer sufficient to establish innocence if their effect was to exert a "disparate impact" upon hitherto excluded minority groups. Given such impact, the employer acquires the burden of proving that his hiring standards, which, although neutral and colorblind, have the necessary effect of excluding minority candidates disproportionately as a "business necessity." Now a "disparate impact" rather than a deliberate intent to discriminate became the basis for official or judicial inference of a violation of Title VII. In turn this led directly into the so-called numbers game, that is, to various statistical tests intended to determine whether the criteria did have a disparate impact. If the finding were affirmative, then obligatory proof of business necessity automatically followed. In turn, the new doctrine of "business necessity" suggested that, absent a strong case, employers might be expected to lower their standards even if their tests were in no way tainted by prejudice and were entirely related to job requirements.

As for the concept of business necessity itself, *Griggs* and later decisions have held that employment tests of any kind (1) must be related to prospective job performance, (2) must serve a reasonable business purpose, such as safety and efficiency, (3) must be demonstrably compelling enough to override their adverse racial impact, and (4) must have no feasible substitute that would be less adverse to hiring prospects for minority groups, even at a somewhat larger expense to the firm.

Besides hiring, another major area of impact of Title VII involves seniority systems. As already noted, discrimination has taken various forms under these systems: separate seniority lists by race or sex, separate departments by race or sex, and closure of promotion ladders by race or sex. Matters become even more complex when, as was the case in basic steel, seniority is departmentally based rather than division- or plantwide. In such cases, if hiring and department assignment have been discriminatory in the past, minority workers will wind up in the least attractive departments. At the same time, they would be unable to use their department seniority to compete for openings in preferred departments. Thus they are "locked in."[7]

More important, they would remain locked in even if hiring and assignment practices are no longer discriminatory. Their present seniority has been made deficient by reasons of past actions. In turn, this raises a very significant question about Title VII: How far does its writ actually run? Is its intent only to terminate *present* discrimination, by compelling revision of hiring, pay, and promotions practices and opening up admissions to unions, training, and apprenticeship programs? Or does its purpose also

---

7 One of the pioneer cases in this field is *United States* v. *Local 189, United Papermakers and Paperworkers, AFL-CIO, CLC;* also *United Papermakers and Paperworkers, AFL-CIO;* and *Crown Zellerbach Corporation* 282 F. Supp. 39 (1968).

include the correction of the present effects of discrimination in the past?

The Supreme Court supplied part of the answer in its *Griggs* decision in 1971. In this case a power company was found to have assigned blacks discriminatorily to a labor department. Later it adopted intelligence and aptitude tests for hiring, promotions, and transfers. Apparently there was no discriminatory intent, although there was an adverse "disparate effect" for blacks. They were locked into the labor department of the company. Thus the Court introduced its double criterion in such matters: (1) the tests must be job-related, and (2) the tests must be justified by a convincing showing of "business necessity."

By this landmark decision, therefore, Title VII was given a degree of retroactive application. The *Bethlehem Steel* case of 1971 [17] posed the problem in another form; in this case the solution was to allow interdepartment transfer by substituting plantwide seniority for department seniority.[8] Vacancies in preferred jobs and departments were thereby opened up for members of minorities. Hiring of candidates from off the street had to wait until these transfers were completed.

In 1977 the Supreme Court again addressed the problem, in a case involving the Teamsters union [10; 16]. Here the Court took a middle-ground position, finding that (1) the employer had discriminated against nonwhites by limiting them to city-driving and servicing jobs, while excluding them from over-the-road work. (2) These employees were entitled to retroactive financial relief where applicable. However, (3) Title VII does not impeach but rather protects the parties' seniority system. A *bona fide* system is not made unlawful even if it perpetuates the effects of discriminatory acts undertaken before 1964, when the act was passed, so long as the system "was negotiated and is maintained free from any discriminatory purpose." (4) Every "post-act" minority applicant who sought an over-the-road job is entitled to relief unless the company can prove that his or her rejection was not for reasons of discrimination.

For nearly ten years, then, or from *Crown-Zellerbach* in 1968 to *T.I.M.E.-D.C., Inc.* in 1977, the Court has established rather firmly the doctrine that Title VII may be applied retroactively to correct the present effects of past discrimination, particularly as regards seniority systems. Thus the phrase "affirmative action" now has acquired a far broader meaning than is almost mechanically suggested in Section 706(g).

THEORY AND PRACTICE IN AFFIRMATIVE ACTION

The core of the expanded meaning of affirmative action involves the use of preferential remedies or quotas based explicitly and deliberately upon race

---

8   For another variant of the problem see *United States* v. *Inspiration Consolidated Copper Co., et al.* [18].

or sex for denominating the class of intended beneficiaries for hiring, promotion, layoff, membership, and other employment practices.[9]

Read strictly, Section 703(j) would seem flatly to foreclose alike all forms of "benign" as well as malign discrimination in employment policies. But this has not proved to be the case. One manner in which benign discrimination has been used over the past several years is through actions of the U.S. Department of Labor based upon Executive Order 11246 and affecting hiring on federally funded construction and other contracts. Here the rationale has been that preferential quotas will increase the employment of "underutilized minorities." A second approach has involved consent decrees in which the courts have approved agreements between the federal regulating agency and employers, and on occasion, unions as well, in which preferential quotas for hiring and promotion are constituent provisions. Indeed, some of these agreements have been consummated without either a finding or an admission of illegal discrimination. Then finally, in some situations where the courts have found unlawful discrimination to be a fact they have ordered reverse discrimination in hiring and promotion as a remedy [11, pp. 51-57].

To date, the Supreme Court has not met the issue of preferential quotas head on. However, it did decide in 1976 that white persons as well as blacks were entitled to the protections against discrimination accorded by Title VII.[10] This indeed could put in question preferential remedies as corrections for past unlawful discrimination.

The case for preferential quotas rests essentially on the principle that the members of the minority class formerly discriminated against have thereby been denied opportunity to find their "rightful place" in the world of employment, that is to say, the place to which their abilities and efforts would have taken them in open competition with others but for a categorical bar that denied them all access. In consequence this "affected class" has suffered pecuniary losses and other deprivations as well. Aiding the disadvantaged as a class thus becomes an appropriate social purpose, while race or sex is a useful concept for grouping persons in the service of that worthy purpose. Among other advantages, this approach will advance the basic objective of full equality, will strengthen the entire community thereby, and will eliminate "stereotyped" views about the working abilities

---

9　Because the races of man are so many and so often are confused with ethnicity, practical official use of preferential remedies has made necessary administrative selection of a small list of groups deemed particularly entitled to such relief.

10　*McDonald* v. *Santa Fe Trail Transportation Co.* [12]. Here the employer fired two white employees for theft while retaining a black who had committed the same offense. The whites successfully used Section 1981 of the Civil Rights Act of 1866 to get into court, which at least tangentially puts preferential quotas in question because implicitly such remedies involve unequal treatment according to race alone. Lopatka [11, p. 54] and [14, pp. 412, 440-441].

of the members of such groups. Further, it is argued that "benign" discrimination of the sorts here envisaged is essential because there exists no practical alternative if the purpose is to cure the effects left over from the past. Moreover, preferential remedies can be expected to be only temporary anyway, it is said, pending the eradication of these past wrongs. Finally, unlike those past wrongs, benign quotas do not place any social stigma upon the young white males who now become the targets of reverse discrimination against them, while the beneficiaries will be "made whole" to some extent in the same process. Indeed, such quotas, by redressing the racial and sex balance at last, will actually serve the ultimate purpose of Title VII, which is that of equal employment opportunity [14, pp. 444-45; 11, pp. 57-58].

Looking now at the case against preferential quotas, it can be argued forcefully that quotas rest upon a denial of the constitutional right to equal protection under the laws. In other words, young white males in particular are singled out as a group to be denied equal employment opportunities, precisely because of their sex and race, and notwithstanding the prohibitions contained in Section 703(j) as well as in the 14th Amendment. Carried further, a young white male seeking his first job and by definition innocent of responsibility for discrimination in the past is asked to stand aside and forego his right to compete on equal terms in his search for his rightful place. Instead, he is to be excluded precisely because of his race and sex, irrespective of his merits. Is it reasonable that he be asked to pay this "tax in kind" for acts in the past with which he had nothing to do and from which he derived no benefits?

So much for the constitutional and statutory arguments. There is also a sociological case, to some extent the counterpart of the one put forward by those who emphasize the benefits of reverse discrimination. It is that even if the intent is "benign," when government discriminates in favor of one class on the basis of race or sex, it necessarily imposes disadvantages upon those excluded by this very discrimination. There is a double consequence from this: Groups are set against each other in a very divisive way, while the beneficiaries themselves become the victims of undeserved contempt because of the help they are accorded as a class, regardless of their merits as individuals. Thus the ancient stigma is reinforced, rather than finally removed.

What this discussion has sought to bring out are the serious problems implicit in attempts to administer Title VII. It is relatively easy to desegregate hiring by requiring that any employment tests relate strictly to the requirements of the job and be requisite to the job if performance is to be acceptable in the sense of essentiality for the safety of workers and equipment and in the sense of efficiency as regards the economic costs of getting the work done.

When we come to the next step, the correction of the present surviving effects of categorical discrimination in the past, the going gets tougher. Should an employer be required to bear the costs of correcting serious educational deficiencies? If he or she is to be compelled to take prescribed quotas by sex, race, or ethnicity, who is to decide the size of the quota? By what standards is it to be set: local population ratios, national population ratios, or other? Is the employer to have the right to reject any of the quota candidates on grounds of ability to do the work? Who is to determine those who are to be included in the quota?

Plainly, these problems are extremely difficult, and inherently so, for in the effort to right the undeniable wrongs of the past, the very source of those past wrongs—exclusion by categorical discrimination—has been officially reintroduced as a remedy.

REFERENCES

1. Arrow, Kenneth J. "The Theory of Discrimination." In *Discrimination in Labor Markets*, edited by Orley Ashenfelter and Albert Rees. Princeton, NJ: Princeton University Press, 1973.

2. Ashenfelter, Orley. "Discrimination and Trade Unions." In *Discrimination in Labor Markets*, edited by Orley Ashenfelter and Albert Rees, pp. 88-112. Princeton, NJ: Princeton University Press, 1973.

3. Becker, Gary S. *The Economics of Discrimination*. Chicago: University of Chicago Press, 1957.

4. Bloch, Farrell E. "Discrimination in Nonreferral Unions." In *Equal Rights and Industrial Relations*, edited by Leonard J. Hausman *et al.* Madison, WI: Industrial Relations Research Association, 1977.

5. Civil Rights Act of 1964, Public Law 88-352; 78 Stat. 241.

6. Glover, Robert W., and Ray Marshall. "The Response of Unions in the Construction Industry to Antidiscrimination Efforts." In *Equal Rights and Industrial Relations*, edited by Leonard J. Hausman *et al.* Madison, WI: Industrial Relations Research Association, 1977.

7. Gould, William B., *Black Workers in White Unions*. Ithaca, NY: Cornell University Press, 1977.

8. *Griggs* v. *Duke Power Company*, 401 U.S. 424 (1971).

9. Hill, Herbert. "Comment." In *Discrimination in Labor Markets*, edited by Orley Ashenfelter and Albert Rees. Princeton, NJ: Princeton University Press, 1973.

10. *International Brotherhood of Teamsters, Petitioner*, v. *United States et al. Daily Labor Report*, May 31, 1977, at D-1.

11. Lopatka, Kenneth J. "Development Concepts in Title VII Law." In *Equal Rights and Industrial Relations*, edited by Leonard J. Hausman *et al.* Madison, WI: Industrial Relations Research Association, 1977.

12. *McDonald* v. *Santa Fe Trail Transportation Co.,* 96 S.Ct. 2574 (1976).

13. Northrup, Herbert R. *Organized Labor and the Negro.* New York: Harper, 1944.

14. Note, "Title VII, Seniority Discrimination and the Incumbent Negro." *Harvard Law Review* 20 (1697): 1260.

15. Oaxaca, Ronald L. "Theory and Measurement in the Economics of Discrimination." In *Equal Rights and Industrial Relations,* edited by Leonard J. Hausman *et al.* Madison, WI: Industrial Relations Research Association, 1977.

16. *T.I.M.E.-D.C., Inc., Petitioner, v. United States et al. Daily Labor Report,* May 31, 1977, at D-1.

17. *United States* v. *Bethlehem Steel Corporation,* 446 F. 2d, 652, 662063 (2d Cir. 1971).

18. *United States* v. *Inspiration Consolidated Copper Co. et al.,* in U.S. District Court of Arizona, Civil No. 70-91-Globe (1973).

Taking Stock   8
and
Looking Ahead

In the preceding chapters, we have reviewed the long history of the American labor movement. We have considered some leading features of its organizational structure. We have examined some of the economic impacts of unionism, and we have looked into some important current issues such as collective bargaining in the public sector and the impacts of the Civil Rights Act of 1964.

The next step is to assess the present position of organized labor, in particular its postwar record of membership growth, its processes of growth, and its prospects for continued growth in the future.

THE GROWTH OF UNIONISM

The Overall Growth of Membership since 1945

In 1945, the total membership of American unions, excluding Canadian affiliates, stood at 14,322,000, or 35.5 percent of all employees in nonagricultural establishments. Table 8.1 provides a summary of the period since that time. Taking the nonagricultural employee group as comprising those most likely to join unions, the most startling fact is the sharp drop in the percentage share of organized labor in the total—from 35.5 percent at the end of World War II to only 24.5 percent 31 years later. Looking at the unions' shrinking relative importance in a little different way, we can say that over the entire period union membership grew by 5.1 million, or by 35.7 percent, while the employee pool from which that membership is drawn soared by 39 million, or by 96.5 percent. The sluggishness of union growth stands out even more clearly when it is noted that less than one out of every eight new workers (13.1 percent) actually joined a labor union during these three decades.

Concentrating upon the most recent period, we find that between 1970 and 1976 union membership rose by only 51,000, while the number of nonagricultural employees jumped by 8.5 million. In other words, for the six years in question, total union membership was virtually stationary.

This recent stagnation also shows up when we look at the private sector alone. In 1970, there were 18.4 million union members in this branch of the economy, and they were about evenly divided between manufacturing and nonmanufacturing. By 1976, the total membership in the private sector had actually dropped to 18.0 million, while the manufacturing component was shrinking by a little over 700,000 members and nonmanufacturing was expanding modestly by 335,000. By contrast, the government sector jumped in membership by almost 1.7 million, almost entirely at the state and local levels.[1]

Table 8.1 U.S. Union Membership, 1945-76.

Year	Total Membership [a] (thousands)	Total Labor Force		Total Nonagricultural Employees	
		Number (thousands)	Union Members (%)	Number (thousands)	Union Members (%)
1945	14,322	65,300	21.9	40,394	35.5
1960	17,049	72,142	23.6	54,234	31.4
1965	17,299	77,178	22.4	60,815	28.4
1970	19,381	85,903	22.6	70,920	27.3
1975	19,473	94,793	20.5	77,051	25.3
1976	19,432	96,917	20.1	79,443	24.5

a. Excludes Canada.

Source: For 1945, U.S. Department of Labor, Bureau of Labor Statistics, *Directory of National Unions and Employee Associations, 1975,* Bulletin 1937, forthcoming. For 1960-76, *ibid.,* "Directory of National Unions and Employee Associations, 1977," as published in *Daily Labor Report* (September 2, 1977), pp. D-14-17.

Before we leave the subject of overall growth, we should note that if we consolidate the figures for union members with those who belong to bargaining associations such as the NEA, it turns out that aggregate membership stood at 21.2 million in 1970 and rose slightly to 22.5 million, or by 6.1 percent, by 1976.

Finally, if we confine ourselves to the years 1974-76, it turns out that total *union* membership alone fell by 767,000, while total membership in unions and associations together dropped by 346,000. Clearly, the verdict has to be that the American labor movement has entered a period of stagnation as far as total membership is concerned, despite the fact that its political influence has never been greater.

---

1   All data from "Directory of National Unions and Employee Associations, 1977," [1].

This disappointing recent record of overall growth requires further comment and interpretation. First, because organized labor in the United States remains so deeply committed to the principles of business unionism, overall growth is of considerably less importance to the individual organizations than it might be to an outside observer. Any particular union is most concerned about its negotiating and strike effectiveness relative to the employers in its own jurisdictional territory. If there are no major gaps in this zone, there is little incentive and actually no need to expand merely for the sake of growth as such.

Second, the declining *relative* position of organized labor since the last war is far more the product of a weight shift in employment patterns and in the composition of the work force than of an absolute decline in total union membership. On the employment side, there has been an explosive growth in the so-called knowledge and service industries and occupations (for example, higher education and computer services). In result, the manufacturing sector, which accounted for nearly 50 percent of the non-agricultural work force in 1955, has dropped to below 25 percent today — not through an absolute decline in employees but through much faster growth in other sectors typically less amenable to unionization. Furthermore, in the recent period the substantial increase in employment in the nonfarm sector has been concentrated among women, teenagers, and part-time employees — groups that have not been easy to organize.

Thus the overall membership figures do not tell the whole story, and while to those who look for a growing labor *movement* rather than growth of particular unions, the postwar record suggests decline; nonetheless, to those concerned with unions as such, the outlook will seem less pessimistic.

Present Centers of Strength and Weakness

Today, American unionism has two kinds of organizational strength: its entrenched positions in manufacturing, construction, mining, transportation, and public utilities; and its already substantial and still expanding wedge in the government sector, particularly at the state and local levels.

In the first category, however, overall membership growth has turned into a small but worrisome decline within the last three years. Partly this reversal reflects the still lagging position of the capital goods industries, despite nearly three years of business recovery. Partly, too, it may be influenced by the migration of industry from the Northeast and Midwest to the Sun Belt and even to the emerging areas of Southeast Asia. In addition, it seems safe to say that the hard goods segment of the American economy may have reached its ultimate limit and thus no longer represents the cutting edge of growth. Finally, there are some signs of employee disillusionment with — or a skepticism about — unionism, although these indications may be dominated by the views of nonunion workers, and hence need to be interpreted with care. A recent poll placed organized labor just above

Congress, which stood at the bottom of the list in public opinion regarding leading American institutions. Moreover, the unions have been losing more than half of recent representation elections and of elections over the decertification of bargaining representation by incumbent unions. And finally, the surge of imports in recent years has brought in its wake a wave of layoffs and plant closures. Very large unions such as the Machinists and the Steelworkers have suffered severe losses in membership from the combined effect of these forces.

By contrast, among union members the disillusionment seems to be directed not against unions as such but against a leadership that is seen as lacking in militancy—a view that partly reflects the increased role of young workers in the membership.

Because government has been a growth factor for unionism for nearly twenty years, it is not surprising that the NEA was the fastest growing organization during 1974-76, and that it is now the second largest labor group in the United States, next to the Teamsters. Equally interesting, among the government unions, AFSCME increased by 469,000 members during those years, to reach a total of 750,000, while the AFT expanded by 321,000, to total 446,000 [1, pp. B-14, B-17].

For the future, it is unlikely that the growth of organizations of government employees can be sustained at the high levels prevalent since 1960, at any level of government. The fundamental reason is that the demand for the services of public workers is unlikely to expand at the high rate characteristic of the last 17 years. For the nation as a whole, public-school enrollment has now reached its peak and may be expected to decline substantially over the next several years. The overall population growth rate is also slowing down, which retards the rate of formation of new local governments as well as the expansion of existing public services provided by local governments already in being. In addition, there is some reason to believe that the creation of new government programs and the imposition of new and higher taxes and bond issues are meeting with increasing resistance from voters. Because of these changes in trend, the best prospects for the government employee organizations would seem to lie in winning recognition in the several states and many local governments where unions and associations so far are hardly even known.

But the task will be difficult, in good part for reasons similar to those that have restricted the ability of unionism in the private sector to move outward extensively from its traditional base in manufacturing, extractive industry, construction, transportation, and public utilities. As in the unorganized private sector, the targets are usually numerous and relatively small, organizing is much more costly, opposition is often intense, the employees are often indifferent or even hostile, facilitating legislation often is nonexistent, and the politicians may see no advantage in helping the union cause.

Patterns of Growth in the Past

The growth of membership has been predominantly centered in the national unions and to a much smaller extent in new local unions. Viewed as a whole, growth can occur in three major ways. The first involves the organization of additional plants or firms in industries that are already largely organized. The second concerns breakthroughs into new industrial territory, followed by further expansion. And the third is simply the passive process of expanding through natural increase in the labor force of the establishments in which the union already has a foothold.

Looking at the history of the national unions can be valuable for understanding the process of growth. For example, consider the Plumbers. Here is an organization built literally from the ground up, through city-by-city formation of independent locals of pipe fitters.[2] By 1889 these locals had joined together to form a national union that affiliated with the AFL in 1897 and had eliminated all rivals by 1914. From thereon, the growth of the union was entirely through natural increase. In recent years, a revived open-shop movement has cut into total membership to some extent.

For a second case, consider the United Steelworkers (USW), a classic instance of what Ulman calls "organizing from the top down" [7, pp. 3-4], initially by breakthroughs into new industrial territory, then by mopping up the still organized plants in the territory, and finally by invading other industries, chiefly by absorbing other unions through merger.

The USW began in 1936 as the Steelworkers Organizing Committee (SWOC). Its founders, John L. Lewis and Philip Murray, had come from the old United Mine Workers. As such they were strong advocates of centralized power and uniform contracts, as in the old Appalachian Agreement as the prototype in bituminous coal. Over its first six years, the SWOC grew through organizing strikes, representation elections, and the capitulation of Myron Taylor of U.S. Steel through his decision to recognize the union. After 1942, the USW grew through natural increase in the steel industry. However, two years later Murray abandoned his cherished principle of one union to an industry by allowing the Aluminum Workers to affiliate with the USW. By 1957, the union began raiding the nonferrous metals industry. In this way it ultimately absorbed the independent Mine, Mill and Smelter Workers (1967), following by taking in the United Stone Workers and the International Union of District 50. In consequence, the USW as a national union has grown in all three ways: through organization after breakthrough, by invasion of new industries, and through natural increase. Mergers also expanded the union and its influence, although obviously they added nothing to total membership of all unions together.

---

2   I have relied extensively on Martin Segal [6] for information on the Plumbers' history and organization.

Our last illustration is the International Brotherhood of Teamsters (IBT). Today the IBT has become a rogue elephant in the American labor movement—a huge, powerful, and isolated organization, existing under constant and growing legal threats, and in reputation accurately perceived as unpredictable and dangerous to encounter.

It was not always this way. In its beginnings, the IBT was as humble and unobtrusive as the Plumbers. Both started from a key occupation, and both began through independent city locals. But the Plumbers stuck to their craft throughout their 90-year history, while the Teamsters were to experience explosive growth, spreading out in so many directions that by 1961 they officially had proclaimed their jurisdiction to be "all workers, without limitation," a variant of the one big union idea.

The IBT was inspired to become a national union and affiliate of the AFL in 1899, at the instigation of Samuel Gompers. But the new organization did not prosper until Daniel J. Tobin began his 45-year presidency in 1909. Until the early 1920s its business was local cartage, drayage, and livery stables. Then the great highway boom got under way, creating a whole new organizing opportunity for the union [5; 3; 2]. In Farrell Dobbs, a brilliant but now forgotten organizer, the IBT found the right man to unionize the over-the-road drivers in the North Central states in 1937. At this stage, the growth of Teamster membership reflected the initial breakthrough, the subsequent mopping up, and then the creation of a rich and powerful base for extending unionization into an incredible variety of fields, from dry-cleaning shops to pallbearing.

These three cases indicate rather well how membership growth has taken place in the past. The next question is: What are the prospects for the expansion of unionism today?

The Challenge of Future Growth

President Meany of the AFL-CIO has recently declared that the organization has no plans for an organizing drive at the present time [4]. Taken at its face value, this would suggest that the federation is not concerned at the recent decline in overall membership. However, to some extent this inference is belied by the current efforts of the AFL-CIO to obtain substantially increased protectionist measures to restrict imports, and to secure changes in the Taft-Hartley Act to make organizing somewhat easier under NLRB procedures.

Nevertheless, the real problem goes much deeper. Except for pockets of nonunion industry in the South and in small towns, manufacturing offers little organizing potential today. This prompts the question, Where is that potential to be found?

The answer seems to lie mainly in the so-called service and knowledge industries, in wholesale and retail trades, and in banking, finance, and insurance. According to each case, the obstacles are many. Many of the jobs call for professional or technical skills held by persons typically not susceptible to the appeal of unionism, particularly of the blue-collar sort. Many of the enterprises are small and therefore do not set manager and managed far apart, with a large and inflexible hierarchy in between. Many of the employees in these fields are young, moved by different values, and unreceptive to the union idea. And, finally, it would probably be far more expensive in organizing and servicing costs per each 100 members for a union to function in these fields.

Thus, while it is too early to formulate firm conclusions about the prospects for renewed overall union growth, it is clear that the outlook is by no means reassuring—at least until new leaders with new organizing techniques appear on the scene. But in saying this, it must be noted at the same time that American unionism remains strong in its present territory, and with its continued emphasis on collective bargaining this strength is what really matters.

FUTURE POSSIBILITIES FOR AMERICAN UNIONISM

Some Contemporary Characteristics of American Unionism

Looking back over the long history of the American labor movement, a few major observations stand out.

One of them is that, to this day, the unions have built their permanence and their success upon their role as market-oriented organizations. In other words, their primary goal has been to improve conditions at the workplace for their members by regulating the employer through contracts negotiated in collective bargaining. In this way, essentially by a process of representative "government" in the unionized industries, workers have acquired a substantial voice regarding the manner in which firms conduct the employment relationship. More than this, the control won through collective bargaining embraces many dimensions besides straight pay rates for the jobs in the bargaining unit. For example, they also include fringe benefits, overtime opportunities, promotions, layoffs, recalls, transfers, premium pay for undesirable hours, disciplinary policies and procedures, union security arrangements; and perhaps most important of all, grievance procedures and arbitration for resolving contested interpretations and applications of rights or obligations contained in the collective agreement. In the large, collective bargaining introduces a system of privately negotiated rules for the joint control of the employment relationship. There are obvious benefits to the employers as well when joint control exists.

Precisely because these contracts, which number now in excess of 150,000 in American industry, are private documents negotiated by persons usually well informed about conditions in the particular firm and its industry and about the problems and interests of both sides, it can be said that, on the whole, this regulatory system has the considerable virtue of being both realistic as well as responsive to the interests of those most closely affected by it. In this respect it differs rather sharply from legislation, which is prepared typically at a distance from its locus of impact and drafted by those who are often uninformed about vital details, in a form made rigid by the necessities of the law itself. Admittedly, collective agreements at times and in part do reflect similar inflexibility, for example, in the wage doctrine implicit to the prototype contract in steel. Still, for the most part labor agreements are drafted mainly with an eye to the local situations from which the bargainers come. In consequence, they are shaped strongly by the environments of their application.

At the present time, there has emerged a broad interest in the Western countries concerning the participation of employees and their unions in the management of the enterprise. The proposals extant range from works committees to seats on the board of directors to profit-financed provision of common shares to the union; at one extreme is "self-management" in the sense of the old proposal of guild socialism in which the employees actually own and manage the firm themselves.

Aside from sporadic attempts at producers' cooperatives from time to time, none of these ideas so far has ever attracted extensive attention in the American labor movement, except for a recent gesture by the United Automobile Workers toward directors' seats in the automobile industry—a gesture that seems not to have been taken seriously by anyone.

The explanation for this seeming lack of interest in labor participation is probably no more than the simple fact that collective bargaining itself is a system of participation of a specialized type. So far, it has worked so well for so long that little need has been felt to explore alternatives. At the same time, however, the *caveat* must be added—and it is a very important one—that the basic reason for the success of the system of collective bargaining lies in the collateral success of the American system of enterprise itself. After all, collective bargaining is at least in part a peculiar kind of profit-sharing system. It works when there are profits to share. Over the lengthy history of American capitalism, generally there have been ample profits available, and so the bargaining system has displayed a continuing vitality. And beyond this, of course, it has executed its regulatory functions with similar effectiveness.

This brings us to a second main observation: Until the advent of the great monetary collapse of 1931-33, American unionism from the inception of the AFL had practiced a peculiar kind of politics—it might well be called the politics of necessity. During this long preceding period, organized labor was a very small minority within the labor force and the larger community—a minority that had to function in an environment that was at best indifferent and more usually hostile. This was no setting in which to undertake a campaign even for the welfare state as viewed in Europe in those days, let alone for some brand of socialism. At the same time, what was the need for such an unpromising endeavor when the system of collective bargaining itself continued to work more than tolerably well already—at least for those employees who were able to enjoy the benefits of unionism?

The answer is obvious: The emphasis continued to be placed upon control of the labor market, because here was an institutional arrangement that worked, and worked well. As for politics and politicians, the rule in those days was simple. Reward your friends, punish your enemies, avoid entangling party alliances, and limit political objectives to narrow supportive legislation such as the restriction of immigration, prevention of sale of prison-made goods, and keeping children off the labor market. Leave the rest to self-organization, the doctrine ran, using collective bargaining to control the labor market and the employers. "Organizational laissez-faire" was the result, in other words, a society dominated by relatively unregulated private organizations consisting mainly of business corporations, with some craft unions sprinkled here and there, and with all of it tied together by an economy of self-regulating markets.

The Great Depression changed all this by forcefully demonstrating the inability of collective bargaining to deal with certain problems of vital interest to working people, in particular, massive unemployment. With the election of 1932, the Democratic party found opportunity to commit the government to active policies for dealing with economic expansion and job creation, and thus to lay the groundwork for an informal alliance with organized labor. Over the ensuing years, this partnership has come to embrace almost the entire labor movement and to display itself repeatedly through candidates, elections, legislation, appointments, and administrative policies. Yet the fact should not be overlooked that the AFL-CIO and its political arm, COPE, always have been most careful to preserve their organizational independence from the Democratic party throughout. To this extent, Gompers's ancient doctrine of nonaffiliation still survives although in truncated form—precisely because such independence provides room and opportunity for bargaining over matters of critical interest to organized labor.

Indeed, there is a parallel here with bargaining with employers as well. By avoiding outright and unconditional identification with the Democratic party, the labor movement retains its independence and increases its ability to extract political concessions. In the case of employers, by limiting themselves to collective bargaining and at the same time avoiding schemes for other forms of participation in the enterprise, the unions elude any responsibility for the profitability of the business. This, too, has its obvious advantages when it comes to making demands and extracting concessions.

In the contemporary scene, then, organized labor stands firmly committed to the politics of the new welfare state, but as for its still central institution—collective bargaining—the outlook remains dominated by an ethic of immediate ends, to be sure, a more complex and a more sophisticated ethic than that expressed by Gompers's famous declaration of "more, and then still more" of 60 years ago, but still a policy of particular pragmatic objectives rather than the pursuit of an overriding and unitary ideology. Thus organized labor still chooses not to undertake a frontal challenge to private business enterprise and sounds no clarion call for a labor party to take the movement into socialism. But will things stay this way?

Permanence or Change in Outlook and Policy

A great part of the answer, I think, will depend upon the future of the American business economy itself. If it can continue to grow according to the trends of the past, then the number of jobs will also increase and real wages will rise, because capital formation has never brought about a rate of labor displacement unacceptable to American unionism as a whole. In other words, most investment has created new jobs and added to productivity. Under these circumstances, the bargaining system can continue to yield the fruits that have entrenched its position for so long. These same conditions would also favor an essentially conservative type of labor leadership, more typical of George Meany and his close associates than, say, of Walter and Victor Reuther, or of Eugene V. Debs at an earlier time.

Also favorable to this view are the differences that still sharply distinguish the American from the British case. For decades, the British unions have had their own political arm in the Labour party, with its now unequivocal dedication to a fully socialist form of society. Buttressing these ambitions is a bitter degree of class consciousness that is the special legacy of British history. At the same time we must not overlook one of the principal sources of that dedication—the overwhelmingly socialist central tradition of the British intelligentsia that has been manifest from the founding of the Fabian Society in 1884. The influence of this powerful group on policy as well as thinking in the union movement, the Labour party, the government, and the civil service is not to be overestimated. And finally, socialism is already a fact in Britain, with the nationalized industries accounting for more than half of the gross national product.

On the surface, at least, the American case appears different in decisive respects. The Democratic party is not a close counterpart to the Labour party. Although the socialist tradition probably predominates among American intellectuals, it by no means has gone unchallenged, and it has never conquered the civil service to the extent typical of Britain. And most important, government-operated industry is still comparatively unimportant, with 85 percent of the GNP still originating from the private sector.

However, the basic question concerns the future of American capitalism itself, for if it should falter and fail, extensive and ever-enlarging measures of state intervention and control would quickly be forthcoming.

In the process, our party politics would then become socialist in fact without bother of accepting the name. With seismic developments of this kind, the labor movement could not escape a parallel involvement and commitment, and a new set of leaders as well.

The way that this could all come about would be through a failure of private capital formation—a failure that would bring in its train a fall or even disappearance of the rate of improvement in labor productivity, a consequent rise in unit labor costs and prices, a decline in the rate of innovation, a retardation in the rate of formation of new jobs, and a continuing, even accelerating, rate of inflation.

The mechanism by which all of this might come about can be considered only briefly here. At the present time, the nation suffers from an unhappy combination of chronic unemployment and chronic inflation; it has now lasted long enough to be termed stubborn and persistent. In consequence the pressures are growing for attacking unemployment through a much larger program of public jobs, to be financed by still larger federal deficits, both on the venerable theory that larger public spending is still the key to the solution of the unemployment problem, because large-scale unemployment can only come from a deficiency of effective demand. Once a program of this form were adopted, say, with a goal of 3 percent unemployment within four years, it would impose a still much greater load of permanent federal financing upon the capital market, and before long an acceleration of inflation would follow. Unemployment would soon rise with this unexpected change in the behavior of the price level. At the same time, increased deficit financing would deprive the private-enterprise sector of the saving essential for continued growth at a time when adjusted real corporate profits after taxes are already below the level of 1966.

In turn, the acceleration of inflation could well bring forth irresistible demands for price controls, which if introduced would make wage controls also inevitable. Once all markets are shackled by controls, rationing and *de facto* government allocations of resources would also become necessary. In such circumstances there can be no collective bargaining. The unions would become wards of the government, along with private business as well. Both would become politicized as the market gives way to decisions by the state.

All this is only a paradigm at the present time. But it does suggest that the destinies of the traditional American labor movement and the American business system are closely bound together, despite the adversary positions of their representatives when they meet at the bargaining table.

REFERENCES

1. *Daily Labor Review,* September 2, 1977.

2. Gillingham, J.B. *The Teamsters Union on the West Coast.* Berkeley: Institute of Industrial Relations, University of California, 1956.

3. James, Ralph C., and Estelle Dinerstein James. *Hoffa and the Teamsters: A Study of Union Power.* New York: D. Van Nostrand, 1965.

4. *The New York Times.* February 24, 1978.

5. Romer, Sam. *The International Brotherhood of Teamsters: Its Government and Structure.* New York: Wiley, 1962.

6. Segal, Martin. *The Rise of the United Association: National Unionism in the Pipe Trades, 1884-1924.* Cambridge, MA: Harvard University Press, 1970.

7. Ulman, Lloyd. *The Government of the Steel Workers' Union.* New York: Wiley, 1972.

Index